Investment Appraisal

C West and N Stein

The Chartered Institute of Management Accountants
63 Portland Place ▪ London ▪ W1N 4AB

First published in 1989, revised 1997 by:

The Chartered Institute of Management Accountants

ISBN 1 874784 57 4

Contents

1	Introduction	1
2	The problem	5
3	Calculating present value	11
4	Net present value and profitability index	17
5	Internal rate of return	23
6	NPV versus IRR	27
7	Payback	35
8	Accounting rate of return	39
9	A basic example	41
10	Inflation	49
11	Taxation	55
12	Sensitivity	61
13	Risk and uncertainty	67
14	Capital rationing	81
15	Test question and solution	85
16	Solutions to practical questions	89
	Appendix: tables of present value factors	95

Chapter 1

Introduction

Investment appraisal is a wide-ranging subject, and as such pervades the four stages of examinations applicable to the Chartered Institute of Management Accountants (CIMA). The contents page shows the scope of this introductory book, which assumes no knowledge of statistics or quantitative analysis techniques. It may therefore be attractive as an introduction to those techniques which are needed for basic investment appraisal. Formulae are avoided as far as possible, with concentration on showing how to solve problems, using simple examples and full calculations and explanations.

The objectives of this book are as follows.

- **To provide an introduction to investment appraisal for students at the earlier examination levels.**

  Of particular relevance to earlier CIMA examinations are the following.

  Stage 1 Cost Accounting and Quantitative Methods (CQM). Syllabus section 2g – Introduction to financial mathematics

  Capital projects have long time horizons, so you must have a sound knowledge of introductory cash-flow techniques, such as net present value (NPV) (Chapters 2, 3 and 4 of this text) and internal rate of return (IRR) (Chapter 5), and how these should be used and interpreted (section 6.1).

  Stage 2 Management Science Applications (MSA). Syllabus section 7c – Applications of financial mathematics

  A key skill of the chartered management accountant is the ability to handle the time value of money, usually with compound interest. The MSA syllabus builds on knowledge gained at Stage 1 CQM. The use of present value tables is necessary for discounting cash flows. You will be expected to be able to compare investments using the criterion of net present value, to know the importance of a positive NPV, and to estimate the approximate internal rate of return. These skills are covered in detail in Chapters 2–5 and in section 6.1.

- **To provide a revision and refresher course to the basic investment appraisal techniques for those at a more advanced stage.**

Of particular relevance to later CIMA examinations are the following.

Stage 3 Management Accounting Applications (MAA). Syllabus section 10b – Project appraisal

Return on investment and its reference to project appraisal is covered briefly in Chapters 7 and 8.

Discounted cash flow (DCF) analysis is one of the most important management accounting techniques. It is used in almost every area of investment, financial and economic appraisal. You should have a detailed grasp of DCF analysis and its main applications (Chapters 2–5).

The NPV of the cash flows arrived at by an application of an appropriate discount rate determines the viability of the project – NPV provides us with an absolute measure of performance. The IRR is the discount rate which when applied to a project gives rise to an NPV of zero – IRR providing a relative measure of performance. Unusual cashflow patterns can give rise to multiple IRRs (sections 6.1 and 6.2).

The comparison of alternative projects can be made using annualised equivalent values (AEV) (section 6.3). The choice of discount rate to be used should be understood and the fact that high risk in a project would require a high discount rate.

MAA examinations will require candidates only to appreciate that a tax payment should be treated as a cash outflow. The computation of tax liabilities will not be examined in MAA. Price changes may feature in MAA examinations (Chapter 10).

Some projects may have an element of uncertainty, and sensitivity analysis is a relatively simple method of appraising risk (Chapter 12).

The text will also provide students at Stage 3 with sound revision material of the earlier two stages.

Stage 4 Strategic Financial Management (SFM). Syllabus section 13c – Investment and decision-making
Aspects of appraisal techniques which must be fully understood include:

- payback, IRR, NPV and how to compare and evaluate each;
- which costs to include in the cash flows;
- how to treat inflation;
- how to deal with capital expenditure and capital allowances;
- how to incorporate working capital expenditure;
- how to adjust for risk.

The text is a useful *aide-mémoir* for Stage 4 as it can be used as a reminder of previous stages and as a revision guide for some of the more advanced techniques covered in the syllabus. The whole text is relevant to Stage 4.

The text can also be used as a reminder to practitioners of the basic concepts and ideas on which to base their own investment appraisal techniques.

The terminology adopted in this book is that of *Management Accounting: Official Terminology* (Chartered Institute of Management Accountants, 1996), and relevant definitions from this appear in boxes in the text.

Throughout the text we shall use a business example based on Bobby Shafto's profitable business. His brother Nobby is to start a business too, and faces similar problems to Bobby. We shall be looking at Nobby's problems in the practical questions at the end of relevant chapters – the solutions to these questions are to be found in Chapter 16.

Chapter 2

The problem

Investment appraisal, in its broadest sense, could be described as being concerned with spending money wisely. We talk of 'investing in a good holiday' in the sense that we expect the benefits or 'returns' from the holiday to be worth more than its monetary cost. Cost-benefit analysis is a technique which can be used to evaluate any investment proposal.

Cost-benefit analysis – a definition

> A comparison between the cost of the resources used, plus any other costs imposed by an activity (e.g. pollution, environmental damage) and the value of the financial and non-financial benefits derived.

This broad type of analysis is outside the scope of this book. Capital investment appraisal is defined as follows:

Capital investment appraisal – a definition

> An evaluation of the costs and benefits of a proposed investment in operating assets. Capital investment appraisal techniques generally involve comparisons between the projected cash outflows to recognise changes in the time value of money, or may be based on unadjusted cash flows.
>
> Discounting methods include: net present value (NPV), discounted cash flow (DCF) yield, also known as internal rate of return (IRR), and discounted payback period. Non-discounting methods include payback period, accounting rate of return, comparative cost, return on capital employed and residual income.

This is obviously a narrower type of investment appraisal, and it is with this type that we shall be concerned. However, we shall not necessarily restrict ourselves to 'operating assets'. For example, investment in an advertising or promotional campaign would be expected to produce benefits which could be evaluated and appraised, and the techniques used in the evaluation would be similar to those used for investment in operating assets.

We shall be considering all the techniques listed in the definition as follows:

- Chapters 4–6: Various discounted cash flow (DCF) methods.
- Chapter 7: Simple and discounted payback.
- Chapter 8: Return on capital employed (ROCE) – for investment appraisal known as accounting rate of return (ARR).

Before we do so, it will be useful to examine a simple problem.

2.1 BOBBY SHAFTO

Bobby Shafto runs a fairly profitable business making buckles. His present return on capital employed is about 15 per cent, and he has maintained a balance at his bank of over £30,000 for some time. A cash-flow forecast, prepared by his accountant, shows that this is likely to be maintained for at least the next five years.

So Bobby wants to put this cash surplus to use by expanding his business to make belts. The current cost of a belt-making machine, including installation, is £25,000, and this machine has an expected life of five years, at the end of which time it will be obsolete and worthless.

Bobby calculates that additional working capital of £5,000 will be required continuously throughout these five years, to finance additional debtors and stocks, and all of this will be released for other uses (e.g., for reinvestment) at the end of the five-year period.

The forecast annual profit and loss account (ignoring inflation) in respect of the proposed belt-making operation is as follows:

	£	£
Sales		40,000
Direct costs (all variable)	18,000	
Overhead costs (all fixed) but excluding depreciation	12,000	
		30,000
Profit before depreciation		10,000
Depreciation of belt-making machine (straight-line basis: £25,000 over five years)		5,000
Net profit (before taxation)		5,000

It is hoped that the actual results will show an improvement on the above forecast figures.

Question

Is it worthwhile for Bobby to expand into belts? In order to gain an overall view of the techniques which can be used in an attempt to answer this question, and of the problems which arise in connection with it, let us make some attempt at answering it, leaving more detailed considerations to the later sections of this book.

2.2 CASH-FLOW POSITION

We can look at the cash-flow position. Bobby will have to expend £25,000 for the machine and £5,000 for the increased working capital, a total of £30,000 almost immediately.

How soon will he get this back? At the end of year 1, he should, subject to fluctuations in the levels of debtors, stocks and creditors, have recovered cash of about £10,000, i.e. the profit *before* depreciation. Note that depreciation is irrelevant for this assessment as the cash outflow occurred when he bought the machine. The same cash-flow recovery applies for years 2 and 3. Therefore, it will be the end of the third year before he recovers his full £30,000.

The simple *payback* period is therefore three years. We shall be considering this further in Chapter 7.

2.3 'PROFIT'

What about his 'profit' in the normal accounting sense? His investment is £30,000, and his 'return' each year is £5,000 (net profit before taxation).

His *return on capital employed* (ROCE) could therefore be calculated as:

$$\frac{£5,000}{£30,000} \times 100 = 16.7\%$$

Note that this time we do charge depreciation, because we are looking at profit, not cash flow as we were with the payback method. Always take great care to ensure that you understand the difference between profit and cash flow, and in what circumstances it is appropriate to apply one or the other concept. Discounting methods almost always require cash-flow figures.

Alternatively, if we regard the machine as a steadily depreciating asset over the five-year period, we could regard his *average* capital employed as £25,000 divided by 2 = £12,500, plus working capital of £5,000 = £17,5000. Note that working capital is not averaged, since it will be required for the whole life of the project. In this case, the ROCE will be:

$$\frac{£5,000}{£17,500} \times 100 = 28.6\%$$

Important note
This average capital employed is the more usual calculation, and should be used in examinations unless otherwise indicated.

ROCE is also known as the *accounting rate of return*. We shall be considering this further in Chapter 8.

2.4 TIME VALUE OF MONEY

No account has been taken so far of the time value of money. We have been treating the cash flows and net profits of year 5 as being of equal value to Bobby Shafto as those for year 1. Obviously cash now is worth more than cash at some time in the future.

In Chapter 3, we shall be looking at the mathematics necessary to make future cash flows equivalent to their present values.

In Chapters 4, 5 and 6, we shall be employing this mathematics in techniques (NPV and IRR) which will, in many ways, improve on the simple payback and ROCE techniques described above.

2.5 INFLATION

What about inflation? Should we adjust any of the figures to allow for the possible effects of inflation on future budgeted cash flows? We shall consider this in Chapter 10.

2.6 TAXATION

What about taxation? The net profit of £5,000 in the annual budget was before taxation, and taxation will obviously affect future cash flows. We shall consider the implications of taxation in Chapter 11.

2.7 SENSITIVITY ANALYSIS

The annual budget for the belt-making operation was obviously based on various assumptions about how the following were likely to behave:

- volume of sales;
- selling prices;
- variable and fixed costs.

Some of these might be considered to be sensitive to market or other forces. A question which might be asked is: 'How far could one or more of these change before the project became no longer worthwhile?' We shall consider sensitivity analysis in Chapter 12.

2.8 UNCERTAINTY

There may be uncertainty about the market for belts, due to insufficient data. Even if there was data available, there could still be an element of *risk* for the project, perhaps due to some unforeseeable change in fashion. These aspects of risk and uncertainty will be briefly explored in Chapter 13.

2.9 CAPITAL RATIONING

Finally, an adviser to Bobby Shafto might come up with alternative uses to which his £30,000 could be put. For some reason or other, perhaps personal, Bobby may not want to borrow extra money to invest in more than one project. On the other hand he might want to do so, but his bank might refuse to lend him the extra money. These restrictions are known as capital rationing and will be considered in Chapter 14.

Chapter 3

Calculating present value

In section 2.4, we said that no account had been taken of the 'time value of money' in the simple appraisal methods we were considering. The basic principle is that £1,000 received now is worth more than £1,000 received at some time in the future.

A sum of £1,000 received now could be invested, say at 10 per cent per annum, in a building society, and in twelve months' time would be worth £1,100, having had £100 interest added. This £1,100, if left invested, and assuming annual compounding (rather than, say, three-monthly or six-monthly compounding) would have 10 per cent of £1,100 = £110 interest added at the end of year 2, and would, therefore, be worth £1,210. We can draw up a table, using year 0 to indicate the present moment, i.e., the start of year 1, and years 1, 2, 3, 4 and 5 to indicate the end of each of those years.

It is usual in examinations (and in practice) to assume that cash inflows *during* a year occur at the *end* of that year. This achieves simplification of the calculations and a 'conservative' approach.

	£	£
Year 0		1,000
Year 1	$1{,}000 \times 1.10$	1,100
Year 2	$1{,}000 \times 1.10^2$	1,210
Year 3	$1{,}000 \times 1.10^3$	1,331
Year 4	$1{,}000 \times 1.10^4$	1,464.10
Year 5	$1{,}000 \times 1.10^5$	1,610.51

The formula for compound interest is $A = P(1+r)^n$

where: A = final amount or compounded sum

P = principal or amount invested

r = annual interest rate, expressed as a decimal, e.g., 10% = 0.10

n = number of years

Looking at the above table, we could also say that £1,331 received in three years' time is worth £1,000 now, or has a *present value* of £1,000, because if we had £1,000 now (rather than wait three years), we could invest it at 10 per cent and have £1,331 in three years' time.

If we wanted to know what £1,000 received in three years' time is worth now, we could calculate it as follows.

$$£1{,}000 \times \frac{£1{,}000}{£1{,}331} = £751.3148$$

and we could check as follows, using compound interest.

	£	£
Year 0		751.31
Year 1	$£751.3148 \times 1.10$	826.45
Year 2	$£751.3148 \times 1.10^2$	909.09
Year 3	$£751.3148 \times 1.10^3$	1,000.00

From this we can produce another table, which shows the present value of £1,000 (and also £1 for convenience) received at the end of individual years, and rounding off the figures to the nearest £1 (for £1,000) and to three decimal places (for £1).

	£	£
Year 0	1,000	1.000
Year 1	909	0.909
Year 2	826	0.826
Year 3	751	0.751

Table 1 in the Appendix to this text shows the present value factors for £1 for a number of future years and at various percentage rates.

Practice

Find the above figures in Table 1.

Discounting could be described as compounding 'going backwards'. The formula is the reciprocal of that for compound interest, i.e.

$$P = \frac{A}{(1 + r)^n} \quad or \quad P = A(1 + r)^{-n}$$

(The use of the negative index ($-n$) in the second version of the formula represents a reciprocal. This form is used in many sets of tables.)

For example:

P = principal or present value
A = final amount received, £1,000
r = annual interest rate, 10 per cent, as a decimal = 0.10
n = number of years, 3

$$\text{Present value} = \frac{£1{,}000}{(1+0.10)^3} = \frac{£1{,}000}{£1{,}331} = £751.3148$$

or £751 to the nearest £, which agrees with the previous calculations above.

Table 2 in the Appendix to this text gives *cumulative* present value factors, or the present value factors for £1 received *annually* for a number of future years (annuities).

For example, for a 10 per cent discount rate:

	Table 1	*Table 2 (cumulative)*
Year 1	0.909	0.909
Year 2	0.826	1.736
Year 3	0.751	2.487
Year 4	0.683	3.170
Year 5	0.621	3.791

(The slight discrepancy in the third decimal place for year 2 is due to the 'rounding off' in these three-figure tables.)

The cumulative table is useful where we need to answer questions such as the following.

Question 1

What is the present value of £1,000 received annually at the end of each of the next five years, using the 10 per cent discount rate?

Solution

Using Table 1, we can calculate:

	£	× factor	= present value (£)
Year 1	1,000	0.909	909
Year 2	1,000	0.826	826
Year 3	1,000	0.751	751
Year 4	1,000	0.683	683
Year 5	1,000	0.621	621
Total present value			3,790

Using Table 2, we can calculate:

	£	× factor	= present value (£)
Years 1–5 inclusive	1,000	3.791	£3,791

Question 2

What is the present value of the following amounts received at the end of each year, using the 10 per cent discount factor?

Years 1 and 2	£1,000 per annum
Years 3, 4 and 5	£2,000 per annum?

Using Table 2, we can calculate:

	£	× cum. factor	= present value (£)
Years 1 and 2	1,000	1.736	1,736
Years, 3 4 and 5	2,000	2.055*	4,110
Total present value			5,846

* The factor of 2.055 is found as follows: deduct the cumulative factor for year 2 in Table 2 from the cumulative factor for year 5, i.e., 3.791 – 1.736 = 2.055. This is, of course, the same as adding the individual factors from Table 1 for years 3, 4 and 5:

	Factor
Year 3	0.751
Year 4	0.683
Year 5	0.621
	2.055

An alternative calculation is possible:

	£	× *cum. factor*	= *present value (£)*
Years 1–5	1,000	3.791	3,791
Years 3–5	1,000	2.055	2,055
Total present value			5,846

Short cuts such as these save time in an examination.

Chapter 4

Net present value and profitability index

4.1 NET PRESENT VALUE OF A PROJECT

We can now return to Bobby Shafto's belt-making project described in Chapter 2, and take into consideration the time value of money referred to in that chapter.

In order to calculate the net present value (NPV) of the project, we must list the cash flows, and multiply them by the appropriate discount factors.

Year	*Detail*	*Cash flow* £	× £	*Discount factor (15%)*	*Present value (£)*
0	Machine purchase	(25,000)			
	+ Working capital introduced	(5,000)			
			(30,000)	1.000	(30,000)
1	Net cash inflow		10,000		
2	Net cash inflow		10,000		
3	Net cash inflow		10,000		
4	Net cash inflow		10,000	2.855	28,550
5	Net cash inflow	10,000			
	+ Working capital released	5,000			
			15,000	0.497	7,455
Total cash flow			25,000	NPV =	6,005

The figure of £6,005 is called the *net* present value because the total initial outlay of £30,000 on both the machine and working capital has been deducted from the sum of the discounted inflows. It represents the estimated immediate change in the value of the business (present value) if the investment is undertaken.

Notes

1. Cash inflows are shown as positive figures, cash outflows as negative figures (in brackets).
2. The cash inflows for years 1–5 inclusive are the forecast profits *before depreciation* (see section 2.2).
3. The working capital figure of £5,000 (see section 2.1) is the sum budgeted to cover the additional finance required for debtors (less creditors) and stocks (raw materials, work in progress and finished goods). If the project finishes at the end of year 5, we can assume that debtors will pay up and stocks will run down to nil.
4. The total of the cash-flow (non-discounted) column is £25,000. This represents the forecast net profit for the period of the project, i.e., five years × £5,000.
5. In the data (section 2.1) we are told that the present return on capital employed (in making buckles) is 15 per cent. The significance of the net present value figure of £6,005 is that the belt-making project would make £6,005 (at the present value of money), more than a 15 per cent yield on the £30,000 capital invested.
6. Normally, this method of appraisal implies that if the net present value is positive, the project should be accepted. If negative, it should be rejected.

4.2 CHOICE OF DISCOUNT RATE

Choice of an appropriate discount rate (15 per cent was chosen in this example) is a controversial matter. Often the weighted average cost of capital (WACC) is chosen.

Weighted average cost of capital – a definition

The average cost of the company's finance (equity, debentures, bank loans) weighted according to the proportion each element bears to the total pool capital. Weighting is usually based on market valuations, current yields and costs after tax.

Illustration

Capital	*Market value, £*	*Rate*	*£*
Equity	8,000,000	× 10%	800,000
Debt	4,000,000	× 8.45%	338,000
Total	12,000,000		1,138,000

Weighted average cost 9.483% (i.e. £1.138 million ÷ £12 million).

An example of how this might be calculated is as follows.

Let us assume Bobby Shafto's capital employed is £90,000. This is composed of:

(a) Debt capital (say a mortgage debenture) of £30,000, with an interest rate of 13 per cent.
(b) Own capital of £60,000, on which Bobby Shafto requires a return of 16 per cent.

The weighted average cost of capital (WACC) would be calculated:

	£		£
Debt capital	30,000	× 13%	3,900
Own capital	60,000	× 16%	9,600
Total	90,000		13,500

$$\text{WACC} = \frac{£13{,}500}{£90{,}000} \times 100 = 15\%$$

An alternative calculation is as follows:

	Rate	*Weight*	*WACC(%)*
Debt capital	13%	$\times$ $^{30}/_{90}$ (33.3%)	4.33
Own capital	16%	$\times$ $^{60}/_{90}$ (66.7%)	10.67
Total			15.00

However, a rate higher than 15 per cent might be chosen if the particular project being appraised is considered to be risky. A risk premium of, say, 3 per cent might be added, making the discount rate 18 per cent. Further consideration will be given to this question of risk in Chapter 13.

Net present value (NPV) – a definition

> The difference between the sum of the projected discounted cash inflows and outflows attributable to a capital investment or other long-term project.

Practice

Using the 'assumptions' above, calculate the WACC.

4.3 PROFITABILITY INDEX

This is a variation on the NPV method of investment appraisal. The calculation required is: divide the NPV of the net cash inflows (*excluding* the original cost of the investment) by the original cost of the investment.

In the case of Bobby Shafto's belt-making project, this would be either

$$\frac{£36,005}{£30,000} = 1.2$$ (if we include the working capital investment at the start as part of the investment), or:

$$\frac{£31,005}{£25,000} = 1.24$$ (if we regard only the cost of the machine as the original investment).

The first alternative seems more realistic.

The profitability index is useful where capital rationing applies, and this will be considered in Chapter 14.

4.4 NOBBY – PRACTICAL QUESTION 1

Nobby has seen his brother's success in the buckle business and wishes to start his own business, making and selling door knockers. He has £44,000 which he wishes to invest in the business. He has the opportunity to invest £40,000 in machinery and £4,000 in working capital. His brother has prepared a forecast profit and loss account ignoring inflation for a ten-year period.

£	£	
Sales		30,000
Direct costs (all variable)	15,000	
Overhead costs (all fixed, includes £4,000 depreciation)	8,000	
		23,000
Net profit (before taxation)		7,000

Nobby would like your advice on the following questions.

1. When will he get his £24,000 back (payback period)?
2. What will his return on capital employed (ROCE) be?
3. If he depreciates the machinery evenly over 10 years, what will his ROCE be on an average basis?
4. What is the net present value of his investment if he wants the same return as his brother currently achieves – i.e. 15 per cent?

Chapter 5

Internal rate of return

5.1 INTRODUCTION

This method of investment appraisal is also known as 'discounted yield' or 'discounted yield rate' or DCF yield or 'discounted rate of return'.

Internal rate of return – a definition

> The annual percentage return achieved by a project, at which the sum of the discounted cash inflows over the life of the project is equal to the sum of the discounted cash outflows.

In simple terms, it is the discount rate which results in an NPV of nil. There are computer programs which will calculate this rate. Some pocket calculators can also be programmed to calculate IRR.

Manual calculation requires trial and error, using interpolation.

5.2 EXAMPLE

We shall illustrate the method by referring to the NPV calculations for Bobby Shafto's belt-making project in Chapter 4. Using a 15 per cent discount rate, the NPV was £6,005 positive. As we use higher discount rates, 16 per cent, 17 per cent, etc., this positive value decreases until, passing through nil, it becomes negative. To find the required percentage we select a higher rate and calculate the NPV at that rate. We could try using a discount rate of 25 per cent as set out below, alongside that for 15 per cent.

Year	*Net cash flows*	*Discount rate 15%*		*Discount rate 25%*	
	£	*Factor*	*PV(£)*	*Factor*	*PV(£)*
0	(30,000)	1.000	(30,000)	1.000	(30,000)
1–4	10,000	2.855	28,550	2.362	23,620
5	15,000	0.497	7,455	0.328	4,920
NPVs			6,005		(1,460)

Using a discount rate of 25 per cent, the NPV becomes *negative*, £1,460. The discount rate at which the NPV is nil is somewhere between 15 per cent and 25 per cent, and obviously it is nearer 25 per cent than 15 per cent.

If we want the IRR to the nearest per cent, we could say that since £6,005 is roughly four times £1,460, then the nil rate is four times further from 15 per cent than 25 per cent.

Rate (%)	*15*	*17*	*19*	*21*	*23*	*25*
NPV(£)	6,000	4,500	3,000	1,500	Nil	(1,500)

This gives a rough answer of 23 per cent for the NPV to be nil.

Accuracy is, strictly speaking, impossible using interpolation since graphically the line joining the two points is not straight (it is, in fact, a slight curve). Fortunately, accuracy is not necessary, since the answer to the nearest 1 per cent is usually adequate.

Figure 5.1 illustrates the calculations required.

Figure 5.1: Calculating nil NPV

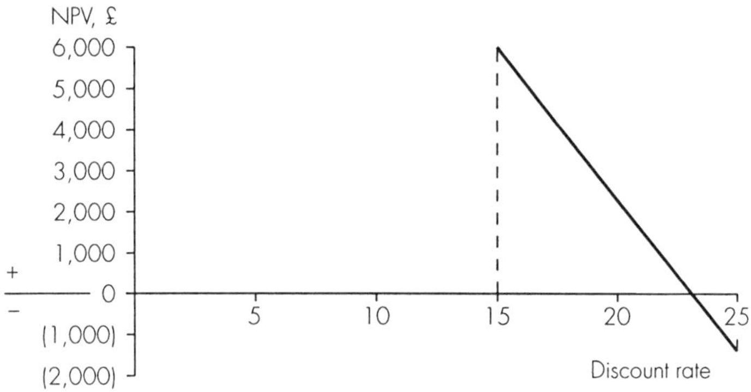

In order to calculate where the line crosses the *x* axis (discount rate), we proceed as follows.

Take the discount rate for the positive value of £6,005, i.e., 15. Add the difference between the positive (6,005) and negative (1,460) discount rates, i.e., 25 – 15 = 10, multiplied by the following fraction;

$$\frac{\text{NPV of 15\% rate}}{\text{NPV of 15\% rate + NPV of 25\% rate}} = \frac{6{,}005}{6{,}005 + 1{,}460}$$

Thus we have:

$$15 + \left[10 \times \frac{6{,}005}{6{,}005 + 1{,}460} \right] = 23.04$$

Note that the greater the distance between the two discount rates chosen (which will give positive and negative NPVs respectively), the less accurate will be the calculated IRR. (This will be illustrated in the basic example in Chapter 9.)

If greater accuracy is required, estimate a starting-point at which the NPV is still likely to be positive, e.g. 20 per cent, and then use trial and error to interpolate between consecutive percentage points, i.e. 20 per cent–21 per cent, 21 per cent–22 per cent etc., until the required yield is obtained.

Before we proceed to a discussion of NPV versus IRR, this is a suitable point to give the definition of 'discount rate'.

Discount rate/cost of capital (capital investment appraisal) – a definition

The percentage used to discount future cash flows generated by a capital project.

Practice

Using the data at the start of Chapter 4, calculate the IRR for the belt-making project, and check your answer with the calculations in this section.

5.3 NOBBY – PRACTICAL QUESTION 2

Using the answer to Nobby – Practical Question 1 (see Chapter 4), calculate the internal rate of return for the door knockers business project.

Chapter 6

NPV versus IRR

Discounted cash flow – a definition

The discounting of the projected net cash flows of a capital project to ascertain its present value. The methods commonly used are:

- yield, or internal rate of return (IRR), in which the calculation determines the return in the form of a percentage;
- net present value (NPV), in which the discount rate is chosen and the present value is expressed as a sum of money;
- discounted payback, in which the discount rate is chosen and the payback is the number of years required to repay the original investment.

Many people (including accountants) find it easier to understand an IRR result (a percentage) rather than an NPV result (a discounted value), and in many cases both methods of appraisal are adequate as an aid in decision-making.

However, there are a number of reservations applicable to the IRR method which should be understood.

6.1 LIMITATIONS OF THE IRR METHOD

NPV and IRR may give different ranking for mutually exclusive projects, i.e. projects of which only one is to be undertaken. An example will illustrate this.

We shall consider another project for Bobby Shafto, e.g. making braces, and compare it with the previous project for belts. The following table shows the figures for belts and braces, together with the increments, or differences, between the two projects.

Note

The initial investment for braces of £30,000 includes £5,000 introduction of working capital, which is released in year 5 (i.e. included in the £25,000 for that year).

Year	*Discount factor 15%*	*Belts Cash flow £*	*Belts NPV £*	*Braces Cash flow £*	*Braces NPV £*	*Increment: braces – belts Cash flow £*	*Increment: braces – belts NPV £*
0	1.000	(30,000)	(30,000)	(30,000)	(30,000)	Nil	Nil
1	0.870	10,000	8,700	3,000	2,610	(7,000)	(6,090)
2	0.756	10,000	7,560	5,000	3,780	(5,000)	(3,780)
3	0.658	10,000	6,580	10,000	6,580	Nil	Nil
4	0.572	10,000	5,720	20,000	11,440	10,000	5,720
5	0.497	15,000	7,455	25,000	12,425	10,000	4,970
		25,000		33,000		8,000	
NPV @ 15%			6,015*		6,835		820
IRR			23%		22%		18.1%

* The small difference of £10 between this figure and the £6,005 we arrived at in the original calculation in Chapter 4 above is due to rounding of the discounting factors – the original calculation used a factor of 2.855 for years 1–4, while using the separate factors for each year results in a total of 2.856.

Belts or braces for Bobby Shafto may be mutually exclusive projects. This may be for several possible reasons:

(a) There may not be enough room in his factory for expanding into both belts and braces.
(b) He may feel that the market will not carry both projects at the same time.
(c) He has the cash for investment in one project, but may be unwilling or unable to borrow for the second project.

Assuming, therefore, that he has to choose between belts and braces, the above table reveals:

Braces (£6,835) has a higher NPV than belts (£6,015)
Belts (23 per cent) has a higher IRR than Braces (22 per cent)

In other words there is a discrepancy in ranking between the NPV and IRR methods.

Note

If the projects were *not* mutually exclusive, both methods of appraisal would show both projects as acceptable.

The reasons for the difference in rankings can be understood by considering Figure 6.1. From the graph it can be seen that below the IRR of the increments (18.1 per cent), the NPV of braces exceeds that of belts. Above that percentage the position is reversed. 18.1 per cent is the IRR of the incremental investment (braces – belts) as shown in the above table.

Figure 6.1: IRR of the incremental investment

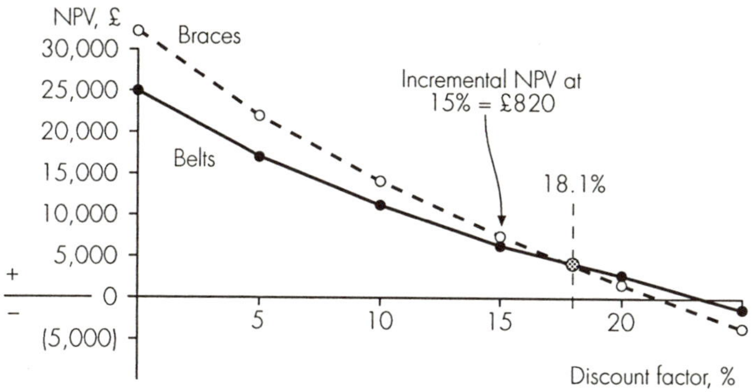

What does this indicate concerning the relative merits of NPV and IRR?

Let us suppose that Bobby Shafto chooses the IRR method of ranking. He will, therefore, choose the belt project, because it has the higher IRR (23 per cent).

We can now ask: 'Is it worthwhile accepting the *incremental* investment?' The IRR is 18.1 per cent (see table above) which is higher than the 15 per cent cost of capital. Therefore it is acceptable.

Belts + Incremental = Belts + (Braces – Belts) = Braces!

Therefore, using the incremental yield approach, we have shifted from belts to braces, which is the preferred project under the NPV ranking.

You will also note that if the cost of capital is greater than 18.1 per cent, then the incremental project is *not* acceptable. Hence, there is no shift from belts to braces. This is confirmed by the fact that the NPV for belts is higher than for braces at all discount factors higher than 18.1 per cent.

Incremental yield – a definition

> A measure used in capital investment appraisal where a choice lies between two projects.
>
> A rate of return is calculated for the difference between the cash flows of the projects.

Practice

Plot you own version of the graph above. You will need the NPV of belts and braces at discount factors of 0 per cent, 5 per cent, 10 per cent, 15 per cent, 20 per cent and 25 per cent. Some of these are already available from the text.

When you have plotted your own graph, compare it with the graph above, and check your figures with the following:

Discount factor (%)	*NPV belts (£)*	*NPV braces (£)*
0	25,000	33,000
5	17,220	22,091
10	11,015	13,552
15	6,015	6,835
20	1,920	1,449
25	(1,460)	(2,880)

6.2 OTHER REASONS FOR PREFERRING NPV TO IRR

(a) Sometimes (though rarely) it is possible for a project to have large negative cash flows not only at the outset but also during its life cycle. This could produce multiple IRRs. NPV curves usually slope downwards (see Figure 6.1), but it is possible for them to be as in Figure 6.2.

Figure 6.2: Multiple IRRs

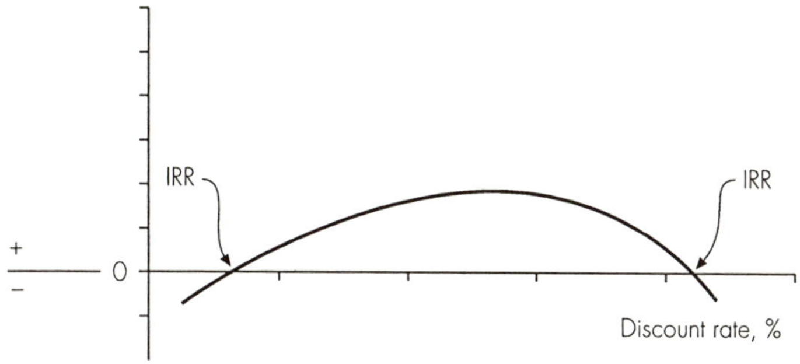

(b) There is a technical reason for preferring NPV to IRR, arising from what is known as the 'reinvestment assumption', i.e., that funds arising from a project are reinvested at the discount rate used for the cost of capital. NPV accords with this, whereas the IRR calculation is based on the assumption that reinvestment will be at the original IRR for the particular project.

(c) Where projects are mutually exclusive, e.g. where there is factory space for only one project, choosing a project on the basis of its IRR alone could result in choosing a project with an investment value of £1,000 and rejecting a project with an investment value of £10,000. This would leave £9,000 which, in theory, could only be invested at the cost of capital. On the whole, NPV is to be preferred to IRR as a method of investment appraisal.

6.3 PROJECTS WITH UNEQUAL LIVES

Normally, projects with unequal lives can be ranked by the size of their net present values or profitability indices (Chapter 4). However, if, for example, there is to be a choice between two machines which do identical jobs, but have unequal lives, then there is a useful technique which can be applied to the net present values.

This technique is called the *annual equivalent cost or value* (AEV), and is calculated by dividing the NPV (calculated in the normal way) by the appropriate cumulative discount factor for the number of years involved. The principle is that the AEV is the constant annual PV, which, if multiplied by the number of years, produces the same NPV as the actual flows.

Example

	Machine A	*Machine B*
Initial cost of machine	£10,000	£20,000
Expected life in years	3	5
Annual running costs	£3,000	£2,000
Discount rate: 12%		

Calculations

Year	*Machine A*			*Machine B*		
	Cash flow	*DF*	*PV*	*Cash flow*	*DF*	*PV*
	£		£	£		£
0	(10,000)	1.000	(10,000)	(20,000)	1.000	(20,000)
1–3	(3,000)	2.402	(7,206)			
1–5				(2,000)	3.605	(7,210)
			(17,206)			(27,210)

Divided by cumulative DF (12%), years 1–3	2.402	
Divided by cumulative DF (12%), years 1–5		3.605
Annual equivalent value	£7,163	£7,548

Machine A has the lower AEV and is therefore preferable.

Question

By how much should the initial cost of machine B be reduced to make it equally attractive?

Solution

The AEV of machine B would have to drop to £7,163. Multiply this by the cumulative DF for years 1–5, i.e. 3.605, which gives £25,823. This is £1,387 (£27,210 – £25,823) less than the present NPV. Since the PV of the running costs will not alter, only the initial cost (discount factor = 1) will alter. Hence the initial cost will have to drop by £1,387 to £18,613. This could be a useful calculation in a competitive situation.

6.4 NOBBY – PRACTICAL QUESTION 3

While considering the door knockers investment, Nobby finds another investment opportunity, this time in door knobs. It also requires an investment of £44,000 which includes £6,000 working capital. This investment is expected to yield the following cash flows:

Year	*£*
1	4,000
2	5,000
3	6,000
4	7,000
5	8,000
6	10,000
7	12,000
8	14,000
9	16,000
10	32,000

The £6,000 working capital is released in year 10 and is included in the £32,000. Nobby is now unsure as to which project to invest in and would like your advice. (Assume that he still requires a return of 15 per cent.)

6.5 NOBBY – PRACTICAL QUESTION 4

Nobby has also been offered two alternative machines with which to make his door knockers, and wishes to know which type to buy (assume a discount rate of 15 per cent).

	Machine 1	*Machine 2*
Initial cost	£8,000	£10,000
Expected life	4 years	6 years
Annual running costs	£2,000	£1,500

By how much would the least preferable machine have to be reduced to make it equally attractive to Nobby.

Chapter 7

Payback

In this chapter and in Chapter 8 we shall consider two *non-discounting* methods of investment appraisal.

7.1 SIMPLE PAYBACK

Payback – a definition

> The time required for the cash inflows from a capital investment project to equal the cash outflows.

Payback is a straightforward and easily understood method, and is therefore very popular. It is commonly used as a first screening method.

We shall use data from Bobby Shafto's proposed projects for belts and braces.

Year	*Belts*		*Braces*	
	Cash flows (£)	*Cumulative inflows (£)*	*Cash flows (£)*	*Cumulative inflows (£)*
0	(30,000)		(30,000)	
1	10,000	10,000	3,000	3,000
2	10,000	20,000	5,000	8,000
3	10,000	30,000	10,000	18,000
4	10,000	40,000	20,000	38,000
5	10,000	50,000	25,000	63,000

If we look at the cumulative cash inflow columns, we can see:

(a) For belts, it is not until the end of year 3 that the cumulative inflows equal the initial outflow of £30,000. The payback period is therefore three years.

(b) For braces, the cumulative inflows equal the initial outflow of £30,000 sometime between the end of year 3 (18,000) and the end of year 4 (£38,000). If we want to be more precise, and, assuming that the cash inflows during year 4 (£20,000) are evenly distributed through the year, then the fraction of year 4 can be calculated by deducting £18,000 (cumulative total at end of year 3) from £30,000 (the initial investment) = £12,000 and expressing this as a fraction of year 4's inflow (£20,000), i.e:

$$3 \text{ years} + \frac{£30{,}000 - £18{,}000 = £12{,}000}{£20{,}000} = 3\tfrac{3}{5} \text{ or } 3.6 \text{ years}$$

Belts, therefore, have a quicker payback period, i.e. the initial cash outflows have been recovered in three years, compared with 3.6 years for braces.

This method of appraisal could be acceptable for very risky projects, where, for example, it is difficult to be confident about the market for a project beyond a very short period. It may also be appropriate for organisations where short-term cash flow is more important than long-term cash flow. But there are serious deficiencies in this method.

(a) It takes no account of the time value of money. For example, for the belts project, the £10,000 inflow for year 3 is worth less than that for year 1.
(b) It ignores cash flows after the payback period. For braces, cash flows after the payback period are much larger than for belts.
(c) If payback is used as the only method of appraisal, it should be possible to accept a project with a negative NPV.
(d) It encourages a short-term view and may discriminate against long-term projects and growth projects.

7.2 DISCOUNTED PAYBACK

This is a slight improvement on the simple payback method. Here are the figures from section 6.1, discounting at 15 per cent:

Year	*Belts*		*Braces*	
	PV	*Cum. PV*	*PV*	*Cum. PV*
	£	*£*	*£*	*£*
0	(£30,000)		(£30,000)	
1	8,700	8,700	2,610	2,610
2	7,560	16,260	3,780	6,390
3	6,580	22,840	6,580	12,970
4	5,720	28,560	11,440	24,410
5	7,455	36,015	12,425	36,835

Discounted payback periods are as follows:

Belts: $$4 + \frac{30{,}000 - 28{,}560 = 1{,}440}{7{,}455} = 4.19 \text{ years}$$

Braces: $$4 + \frac{30{,}000 - 24{,}410 = 5{,}590}{12{,}425} = 4.45 \text{ years}$$

What does this tell us? Very little more than that both belts and braces have positive NPVs and that both payback periods are less than five years; that belts has a slightly shorter discounted payback period than braces, and that braces (incidentally) has the greater NPV.

However, there could be a good case for calculating the simple payback periods for projects *as well as* the NPVs. A project could have a positive NPV but a long simple payback period, which could make the project unacceptable, e.g. because of the strain this might have on the liquidity of the organisation.

This brings us to a very important point. The methods of investment appraisal covered in this book should not be considered in isolation. Management accounting techniques are tools which the accountant can use to present information to management to assist them in decision-making. There are other techniques which can be used, and other factors which may need to be taken into consideration.

For example, the NPV and the payback periods of the belt-making machine may be acceptable in the sense that they meet the criteria set by Bobby Shafto. But Bobby may decide against it on the following grounds:

(a) When a break-even analysis is applied to the project, the break-even point may be too high, i.e. the margin of safety may be unacceptable; and
(b) the machine may create too much noise or pollution.

Chapter 8

Accounting rate of return

This is another 'non-discounting' method of appraisal which springs from the use of return on capital employed (ROCE) as the 'prime ratio' in financial analysis.

This has been briefly considered in section 2.3. The usual method of calculation is to express average annual pre-tax profit as a percentage of the *average* 'capital employed', i.e. the original investment.

In the case of belts and braces, the calculations are:

		Belts	*Braces*
			£ £
Total pre-tax profit for five years		25,000	33,000
Average annual pre-tax profit		5,000	6,600
Average capital employed:			
Machines: £25,000/2 =	12,500		
Working capital	5,000		
		17,500	17,500
Accounting rate of return		28.6%[1]	37.7%[2]

Notes:

1. $\frac{5{,}000 \times 100}{17{,}500}$

2. $\frac{6{,}600 \times 100}{17{,}500}$

This method provides useful additional information, particularly if an organisation is concerned with profits rather than liquidity. It is a poor method of appraisal, and certainly should not be used as a sole method of appraising a project, since it suffers from two major defects:

(a) it takes no account of the time value of money.
(b) It takes no account of the timing of the profits, since it is based on an 'average' calculation.

For example, consider the following:

	Project X	*Project Y*
	£	£
Investment	10,000	10,000
Profit year 1	1,000	3,000
2	2,000	2,000
3	3,000	1,000
Total profit	6,000	6,000
Average annual profits	2,000	2,000

The ARR is the same for both projects (£2,000 × 100) ÷ (£10,000/2), i.e., 40 per cent, but project Y is clearly preferable for the timing of the profits.

Accounting rate of return – a definition

$$\frac{\text{Average annual profit from an investment}}{\text{Average investment}} \times 100$$

Sometimes used in investment appraisal, and a form of return on capital employed. Unlike net present value and internal rate of return, the ratio is based on profits, not cash flows. Exclusive use of this ratio is not recommended.

This is as far as you are likely to have to go for the more basic examinations. Attempt the basic example in the next section to consolidate your knowledge in any case, then proceed to Chapters 10–15 if your syllabus requires it.

Chapter 9

A basic example

The following example is suitable for all students studying for the earlier examinations which include the basics of investment appraisal, and is also good revision practice for those who have progressed to the more advanced levels.

The question is based on a question from the Institute of Bankers Banking Diploma paper in Accountancy (Stage 2). The original question has been slightly expanded to cover payback, accounting rate of return and IRR.

9.1 QUESTION

The directors of Vetch Ltd are considering whether to undertake either of two mutually exclusive investment appraisal projects at a cost of £500,000. It is intended to finance the project as follows.

	£000	*Cost*
Equity finance	300	20%
Bank loan	200	12%
	500	

The cash flows associated with the two projects have been estimated as follows:

		Project A	*Project B*
Cash flows		*£000*	*£000*
Initial investment		500	500
Cash inflows:	Year 1	200	400
	Year 2	300	200
	Year 3	200	200
	Year 4	400	200

You are required to:

(a) calculate the weighted average cost of capital (WACC) for either of these projects to the nearest whole per cent;
(b) calculate the payback period (non-discounted) of each project.
(c) calculate the accounting rate of return of each project;
(d) calculate the net present value of each project using a WACC of 17 per cent;
(e) calculate the internal rate of return of each project;
(f) advise management which project it should undertake.

Assume that the initial investment will occur immediately and that cash inflows will occur at the end of each year. Ignore taxation.

Present value tables to assist in the calculations are set out in the Appendix to this text. The calculation of the WACC required in part (a) of the question is not examinable until Stage 4. However, the calculation is not difficult in this case so it has been left in the question.

Discussion

Two assumptions need to be made in answering this question:

(a) that the investment is in fixed assets only, with no requirement for working capital;
(b) that the value of the fixed assets at the end of the project is nil.

In answering examination questions it is wise to state any such assumptions at the beginning of your answer.

9.2 SOLUTION

(a) **Weighted average cost of capital** (see section 4.2)

	Cost (%)	*Weight*	*WACC*
Equity	20	$\times$ $^{300}/_{500}$ (60%) =	12.0
Bank loan	12	$\times$ $^{200}/_{500}$ (40%) =	4.8
			16.8

i.e. 17% to the nearest *whole* value.

(b) **Payback period (non-discounted)** (see Chapter 7)

	Project A	*Project B*
Cumulative cash inflows	*£000*	*£000*
Year 1	200	400
Year 2	500	600

The payback period is the point in time when inflows equal the initial investment of £500,000.

For project A it is therefore two years.

For project B it is:

$$1 \text{ year} + \frac{500 - 400}{600 - 400} = 1.5 \text{ years}$$

(c) **Accounting rate of return (ARR)** (see Chapter 8)

	Project A	*Project B*
	£	*£*
Calculate the average capital employed (see section 2.3) £500,000/2 =	250,000	250,000
Calculate the profits of each project (cash inflows = profit *before* depreciation) Assume the initial investment is fully depreciated over the four years:		
∴ total inflows	1,100,000	1,000,000
less: investment (= depreciation)	500,000	500,000
Total profit for four years	600,000	500,000
Calculate the average annual profit for each project, i.e. divide above profits by four years	150,000	125,000
Express the average annual profits as a percentage of average capital employed:		
Project A: 150,000/250,000 × 100	60%	
Project B: 125,000/250,000 × 100		50%

(d) **Net present value (NPV)** (see Chapter 4)

Use WACC as calculated in part (a) of this solution.

Year	*Factor*	*Project A*		*Project B*	
	17%	*Cash flow*	*PV*	*Cash flow*	*PV*
		£	£	£	£
0	1.000	(500,000)	(500,000)	(500,000)	(500,000)
1	0.855	200,000	171,000	400,000	342,000
2	0.731	300,000	219,300	200,000	146,200
3	0.624	200,000	124,800	200,000	124,800
4	0.534	400,000	213,600	200,000	106,800
Net present values:			228,700		219,800

(e) **Internal rate of return (IRR)** (see Chapter 5)

This can be calculated by interpolation. For each project, a discount rate should be chosen that is likely to give a negative NPV. In view of the high NPVs, discount rates are likely to be high. Trial of several rates may be necessary before one is found that gives a negative NPV, and in view of the distance from the original rate of 17 per cent, it will also be necessary to find a nearer positive rate. The reason is that interpolation between rates which are far apart leads to unacceptable error – the line of interpolation is a curve rather than a straight line. This error is acceptable only between discount rates which are reasonably close. The figures which give the best results are as follows.

Project A

Year	*Cash flows*	*Factor*	*PV*	*Factor*	*PV*
	£	*35%*	£	*40%*	£
0	(500,000)	1.000	(500,000)	1.000	(500,000)
1	200,000	0.741	148,200	0.714	142,800
2	300,000	0.549	164,700	0.510	153,000
3	200,000	0.406	81,200	0.364	72,800
4	400,000	0.301	120,400	0.260	104,000
Net present values			14,500		(27,400)

By interpolation between these two rates:

$$\text{IRR} = 35 + \left[\frac{14{,}500}{14{,}500 + 27{,}400} \times (40 - 35) \right] = 35 + (0.346 \times 5) = 36.73\% \approx 37\%$$

Project B

Year	*Cash flows*	*Factor*	*PV*	*Factor*	*PV*
	£	*40%*	*£*	*45%*	*£*
0	(500,000)	1.000	(500,000)	1.000	(500,000)
1	400,000	0.714	285,600	0.690	276,000
2	200,000	0.510	102,000	0.476	95,200
3	200,000	0.364	72,800	0.328	65,600
4	200,000	0.260	52,000	0.226	45,200
Net present values			12,400		(18,000)

By interpolation between these two rates:

$$\text{IRR} = 40 + \left[\frac{12{,}400}{12{,}400 + 18{,}000} \times (45 - 40) \right] = 40 + (0.408 \times 5) = 42.04\% \approx 42\%$$

Notes

1. To save time, the cumulative tables could have been used for years 2, 3 and 4 for project B, e.g.

   Discount rate 40%:

Years 1–4	factor 1.849
Less year 1	factor 0.714
Therefore years 2–4	factor 1.135

   £200,000 × 1.135 = £227,000
   (£102,000 + £72,800 + £52,000 = £226,800. The difference is due to rounding off in the three-figure DCF tables.)

2. If pressed for time in an examination, the above might take too long. Since the IRR figures are high, the degree of accuracy is not critical. If, for example, for project A you had tried the 35 per cent rate (NPV = £14,500), it might save time to say that the IRR was slighly over 35 per cent.

Summary (not necessary in examination answers, unless time permits)

		Project A	Project B
(a) WACC	17%		
(b) Payback		2 years	1.5 years
(c) ARR		60%	50%
(d) NPV		£228,700	£219,800
(e) IRR		37%	42%

(f) **Advice to management**

It is difficult to advise management on which of these two mutually exclusive projects it should undertake.

NPV is usually considered to be the most reliable method of ranking, but in this case both the projects have high NPVs, and the NPV of project A is only slightly higher than that for project B. The ranking shown by IRRs is not reliable (see note below).

If there are no other criteria which management may wish to use to choose between the projects, then project B would seem to have the edge because of its shorter payback period (1.5 years compared with two years for project A) – particularly if the projects were 'risky', then £400,000 cash inflow in year 1 for project B is double that for project A.

Note re IRR ranking

This would not be expected in the solution to the question as set (see section 6.1).

Calculate the incremental cash flows:

Year	*A* £	*B* £	*Increment A–B* £	*Discount rate 17%*	*PV* £
0	(500,000)	(500,000)	–	1.000	–
1	200,000	400,000	(200,000)	0.855	(171,000)
2	300,000	200,000	100,000	0.731	73,100
3	200,000	200,000	–	0.624	–
4	400,000	200,000	200,000	0.534	106,800
	600,000	500,000	100,000	NPV	8,900

Calculate the IRR by interpolation:

Year	*Increment A–B* £	*Try disc. rate 20%*	*PV* £
0	–	1.000	–
1	(200,000)	0.833	(166,600)
2	100,000	0.694	69,400
3	–	0.579	–
4	200,000	0.482	96,400
	100,000	NPV	(800)

$$\text{IRR} = 17 + \left[\frac{8{,}900}{8{,}900 + 800} \times (20 - 17) \right] = 19.75\%$$

IRR and NPV are contradictory below 19.75 per cent (e.g. at 17 per cent, the WACC in this question), but would not be contradictory above 19.75 per cent.

Chapter 10

Inflation

We can define inflation simply as an increase in prices (similarly deflation can be defined as a fall in prices).

Inflation can give rise to two problems in investment appraisal:

1. its effects on future cash flows; and
2. its effects on the discount rate used.

In recent years the rate of inflation has dropped, but inflation can still be an important factor when considering investment for the future.

Inflation will be either general or specific. General inflation refers to the increase of a whole range of goods – such as the retail price index (RPI) measures. Thus the RPI is an index of *general* inflation. Specific inflation, on the other hand, is an increase in the price of a particular item (or a group of similar items), such as wages, materials, etc.

Very briefly, it can be stated that inflation cancels out, but only when the rate of inflation is the same for all cash inflows (sales revenue, etc.) and cash outflows (materials, labour, all types of overhead), sometimes referred to as synchronised inflation or non-differential inflation.

It is interesting to consider why non-differential rates of inflation cancel out. We shall use Bobby Shafto's belt-making project as an example. In order to allow for inflation at, say, 5 per cent over the next five years, we shall have to do two things.

(a) Increase the cash flow figures to allow for this, e.g.:

Year 1 £10,000 $\times$ 1.05
Year 2 £10,000 $\times$ $(1.05)^2$
Year 3 £10,000 $\times$ $(1.05)^3$

and so on...

A 5 per cent inflation rate is, of course, compound, since it is usually expressed as an annual rate, with each year increasing by a percentage rate on the previous year.

(b) Increase the discount rate by the assumed rate of inflation, i.e.:

$$15\% \text{ increased by } 5\% = \frac{1}{1.15 \times 1.05}$$

The calculations for the belt-making project will therefore be:

Year	*Cash flow*	×	*Discount factor*
0	$(30{,}000) \times 1$		1
1	$10{,}000 \times 1.05$		$\frac{1}{(1.15) \times (1.05)}$
2	$10{,}000 \times (1.05)^2$		$\frac{1}{(1.15)^2 \times (1.05)^2}$
3	$10{,}000 \times (1.05)^3$		$\frac{1}{(1.15)^3 \times (1.05)^3}$
4	$10{,}000 \times (1.05)^4$		$\frac{1}{(1.15)^4 \times (1.05)^4}$
5	$10{,}000 \times (1.05)^5$		$\frac{1}{(1.15)^5 \times (1.05)^5}$

It can be seen that the inflation factors cancel out, e.g.:

$$\text{For year 1: } \frac{10{,}000 \times 1.05}{1.15 \times 1.05} = \frac{10{,}000}{1.15} = £8{,}700$$

This means that the NPV will be the same as calculated without inflation, £6,015 (as shown in section 6.1).

We must appreciate that there are two different rates used in discounting depending on circumstances: the money rate (market or nominal rate) and the real rate (consumption or purchasing power rate). The money rate allows for inflation, the real rate is the money rate less the effect of inflation.

Where there are differential inflation rates in the appraisal – for example, where wage rates are expected to have a higher rate of increase than other costs and the sales prices – then inflation must be taken into account, with the cash-flow figures adjusted accordingly. It is important that the discount rate is also adjusted.

The Fisher Effect is described in a formula which was developed to take account of the relationship found between the real, inflation and money rates:

(1 + real rate of interest) × (1 + inflation rate) = (1 + money rate of interest)

If we ignore inflation for the present, then everything discounted in the past was at the real rate of interest, or a rate of interest applicable at times of zero inflation. In other words, in times of zero inflation, we can look at rate of growth in an investment as its increase in purchasing power, i.e. its real value in real terms. If, for instance, you had £500 today which you were prepared to loan to someone for a year (without inflation), you would expect to get back that £500 plus some form of increase in its value to pay you for the loss of use of that money for the year.

In times of inflation, the rate of inflation has to be taken into account to provide for not only the loss of that £500 for one year, but also for its reduction in purchasing power in that year. When we combine both in this manner, we have the money rate of interest.

The real rate of interest in terms of the time value of money looks at purchasing power, whereas the money rate of interest looks at time value of money in cash terms. It is important that we use the correct discount rate, i.e. the real rate should be used only where real cash flows are given (where inflation has already been taken out). The money rate should be used only when cash flows including inflation are given.

Where inflation is present, we can either:

1. take the money cash flows and discount them by the money rate of interest; or
2. take the money cash flows and discount them by the rate of inflation (giving you the real cash flows) and then discount the real cash flows by the real rate of interest.

Both methods will produce exactly the same result.

Look again at Bobby Shafto's belt-making project, and assume that there is general inflation of 5 per cent. However, specific inflation is increasing his sales revenue by 3 per cent per annum and his variable costs by 6 per cent per annum. His fixed costs are also increasing by 4 per cent per annum.

The first stage here is to inflate all the revenues and costs by their own inflation rate, then find the net cash flow (which will now be stated in money cash flow terms). Assume that the investment of working capital stays constant throughout.

Year	*Sales revenue*	*Inflation*	*Money cash flow*	*Variable costs*	*Inflation*	*Money cash flow*	*Fixed costs*	*Inflation*	*Money cash flow*
1	40,000	1.03	41,200	18,000	1.06	19,080	12,000	1.04	12,480
2	40,000	1.03^2	42,436	18,000	1.06^2	20,225	12,000	1.04^2	12,979
3	40,000	1.03^3	43,709	18,000	1.06^3	21,438	12,000	1.04^3	13,498
4	40,000	1.03^4	45,020	18,000	1.06^4	22,725	12,000	1.04^4	14,038
5	40,000	1.03^5	46,371	18,000	1.06^5	24,088	12,000	1.04^5	14,600

Year	*Net money cash flow*
1	9,640
2	9,232
3	8,773
4	8,257
5	7,683

The next stage is to find the NPV using the money rate of interest.

Year	*Net money cash flow* £	*Money rate disc. factor* 20.75%	*Present value* £
0	(30,000)	1.000	(30,000)
1	9,640	0.828	7,982
2	9,232	0.686	6,333
3	8,773	0.568	4,983
4	8,257	0.470	3,881
5	12,683	0.390	4,946
		NPV =	(1,875)

(Year 5 includes the £5000 working capital released)

The money rate discount factor used above was produced from the real rate × the general inflation rate, i.e.:

$1.15 \times 1.05 = 1.2075 - 1 = 20.75\%$

We shall now prove that the same result will be arrived at by the alternative method of using first the general inflation rate of interest, and then the real rate of interest on the resultant cash flows (real cash flows).

Year	Money cash flow £	General inflation rate 5%	Real cash flows £	Real discount rate 15%	Present value £
0	(30,000)	1.000	(30,000)	1.000	(30,000)
1	9,640	0.952	9,177	0.870	7,984
2	9,232	0.907	8,373	0.756	6,330
3	8,773	0.864	7,580	0.658	4,988
4	8,257	0.823	6,796	0.572	3,887
5	12,683	0.784	9,943	0.497	4,942
				NPV =	(1,869)

The difference is due to roundings.

If differential interest rates are *not* anticipated, then inflation adjustments should be omitted from *all* the calculations. However, it should be pointed out that differential rates of inflation are almost inevitable, and that the retail price index is only a crude guide. On the other hand, forecasting differential rates (or forecasting the RPI for that matter) is, to say the least, a difficult task. Whether or not to make the attempt, or ignore inflation altogether on the grounds that it will broadly cancel out, is dependent on the circumstances surrounding the particular project appraisal.

Chapter 11

Taxation

The inclusion of taxation in cash flows is no more than correcting the cash flows to accord with the anticipated facts. Taxation payments are cash outflows, just as wages, material purchases, etc., are. It is particularly important to allow for taxation when using DCF methods.

The taxation effects which need to be reflected in investment appraisal are:

(a) capital allowances;
(b) corporation tax on inflows;
(c) government grants;
(d) discounting rate post-tax.

11.1 CAPITAL ALLOWANCES

The main capital allowances relevant for our purposes are:

- *Plant and machinery* 25 per cent annual writing-down allowances (reducing balance basis). The Finance Act 1997 introduced a 6 per cent rate (reducing balance) for plant with an expected life when new of 25 years or more. The new rate applies only to businesses spending more than £100,000 a year or more on such assets.
- *Industrial buildings* 4 per cent annual writing-down allowances (straight-line basis).

On the sale of an industrial building a balancing charge or allowance will arise. This will effectively mean a tax charge or reduction in the year following the sale, equal in most cases to corporation tax on the difference between sale proceeds and the written-down value.

If an industrial building is sold for more than its original cost, a capital gains tax charge may arise.

On the sale of plant and machinery things are not so simple, because purchases may be pooled with other items, so that a balancing adjustment may not arise. There are three main possibilities when the plant is pooled and sold at the end of the project:

(a) Sale proceeds are less than cost of the asset but exceed the written-down value. In this case, sale proceeds will be deducted from the pool so that future capital allowances on plant remaining in the pool will be less than they would have been without the project under review.
(b) Sale proceeds are less than the tax written-down value. The deduction of sales proceeds from the pool will leave a residue of expenditure in the pool, thus increasing future capital allowances.
(c) Sale proceeds exactly equal the tax written-down value. In this case there will be no tax effect because the amount deducted from the pool as sale proceeds will exactly equal the balance in the pool for the assets concerned.

In all three cases the proceeds of sale should be shown as a cash inflow in the year of sale. In cases (a) and (b) it is also necessary to include an outflow or inflow to reflect the continuing effect on future capital allowances. It is unlikely that examination questions will require the calculation of these figures.

In the third case there is no tax effect and no further adjustment is necessary. Remember, however, that the proceeds of sale still come in as an inflow.

Before we leave capital allowances, it is necessary to consider one further possibility, 'de-pooling'. De-pooling means that plant with a life of up to five years may be excluded from the pool and the capital allowances calculated separately. On the sale of such assets within the five-year period a balancing charge or allowance arises.

11.2 OTHER TAXATION EFFECTS

(a) Corporation tax on inflows: forecast inflows will attract a tax charge at the appropriate rate payable nine months after the year end.

(b) Government grants: any government grants receivable must be accounted for in the appropriate period.
(c) Discounting rate: a post-tax discounting rate should be used.

11.3 EXAMPLE

Here is an illustration based on the belt-making project. We shall assume that the machine attracts an annual writing-down allowance (WDA) of 25 per cent and that the de-pooling election was made, thus giving rise to a balancing allowance at the end of the project. We shall also assume that Bobby Shafto is a company paying corporation tax at full rate of 33 per cent.

We must first calculate the capital allowances.

		Allowances at 33%
	£	£
Belt-making machine	25,000*	
Year 1 WDA 25%	6,250	2,062
	18,750	
Year 2 WDA 25%	4,687	1,547
	14,063	
Year 3 WDA 25%	3,516	1,160
	10,547	
Year 4 WDA 25%	2,637	870
	7,910	
Year 5 WDA 25%	1,978	653
	5,932	
Year 6: scrapped, proceeds	–	
Balancing allowance	5,932	1,958
		8,250

* The cash-flow figures which follow allow for the working capital requirement of £5,000 in year 0.

We may now tabulate the cash flows, assuming that the tax effects flow through one year after the income or expenditure to which they relate (see note at the end of this section).

For example, the tax payable in year 2 is based on the profit (before depreciation) = cash inflow, less the capital allowances for year 1 (i.e., £3,500 – £2,062 = £1,438).

In examination questions the date of capital expenditure, designated 'year 0', is often stated to be the first day of an accounting period. The expenditure thus qualifies for capital allowances in year 1, and the cash-flow benefit derived from the capital allowances begins in year 2, assuming that there is a one-year delay on tax payments. It could be, however, that the expenditure could actually occur in the previous financial year, thus bringing forward the benefit of the capital allowances to year 1. Read the question carefully for information about the dates of expenditure. In the absence of information to the contrary, it is probably best to proceed as in the example below, in which benefit is assumed to begin in year 2.

It is convenient to calculate the tax effects separately, as shown below.

Year	*Cash outflow*	*Cap. all'nces @ 33%*	*Cash inflow*	*CT at 33%*	*Net cash flow*	*Disc. fact. 15%*	*Present value*
	£	£	£	£	£	£	£
0	(30,000)	–	–	–	(30,000)	1.000	(30,000)
1	–	–	10,000	–	10,000	0.870	8,700
2	–	2,062	10,000	(3,300)	8,762	0.756	6,624
3	–	1,547	10,000	(3,300)	8,247	0.658	5,427
4	–	1,160	10,000	(3,300)	7,860	0.572	4,496
5	–	870	15,000*	(3,300)	12,570	0.497	6,247
6	–	653	–	(3,300)	(2,647)	0.432	(1,144)
7	–	1,958	–	–	1,958	0.376	736
	(30,000)	8,250	55,000	(16,500)	16,750		1,086

The cross-cast should be checked to prove the correctness of the net cash-flow figure of £16,750.

* Including recovery of £5,000 working capital.

Ir can be seen that the incidence of taxation reduces the NPV from £6,015 (see section 6.1) to a mere £1,086.

There are occasions where the tax benefits calculated to flow from the project in one year exceed the tax charge relating to the project for that year. In the example we have just been looking at, there is a tax benefit in year 7 of £1,958 flowing from capital allowances, but there is no tax payable in year 7 since there is no cash inflow (profit before depreciation) in year 6. If we assume that this project (belt-making) is additional to other profitable activities of the firm (e.g. buckles), then the allowance could be offset against those other profits. In this case, the calculation can proceed as usual, with a tax benefit of £1,958 being shown as a positive net cash flow in year 7. In other words, the belt-making product produces, in year 7, a tax benefit for the whole organisation. If, however, there were no other profits against which the allowance could be offset, then it would be carried forward to a year when it could be offset.

Practice

Using the data for Bobby Shafto's belt-making project together with the given rates for writing-down allowance and corporation tax, calculate the revised NPV for the project including taxation.

Compare your answer with the calculations in this section.

Chapter 12

Sensitivity

12.1 INTRODUCTION

Sensitivity analysis is a relatively simple method of appraising risk. There are other more sophisticated methods which are discussed in Chapter 13. Sensitivity is discussed separately here because it is sometimes singled out for 'basic' level examinations, whereas other methods are usually considered more 'advanced'.

In section 2.7, we said that the annual budget for the belt-making operation was obviously based on various assumptions about the likely behaviour of sales volumes, selling prices, variable costs, project life, initial outlay and cost of capital. The purpose of the analysis is to help managers assess how the NPV may be altered by the sensitivity to change of any of these factors which were used in the original calculations of cash flows for the project.

For example, if sales volume were considered to be the most sensitive factor, subject to variations ±10 per cent, then the NPV could be recalculated to show the best or worst position.

Sensitivity analysis – a definition

> A modelling and risk-assessment procedure in which changes are made to significant variables in order to determine the effect of these changes on the planned outcome. Particular attention is thereafter paid to variables identified as being of special significance.

12.2 EXAMPLE

In order to illustrate how this can be achieved, we shall simplify the belt-making project data, excluding the introduction of working capital (purely to simplify the calculations), and assuming all costs to be 'variable' or 'avoidable'.

Annual budget:	£
Sales: 40,000 units at £1	40,000
Variable costs: 40,000 units at 75p	30,000
Net cash flows	10,000
Initial outlay	25,000
Life of project	5 years
Cost of capital	15%
Present value of cash flows: £10,000 × 3.352	33,520
Less: Initial outlay	25,000
Therefore NPV is	8,520

Note: the factor of 3.352 is obtained from Table 2 in the Appendix to this text, as explained in Chapter 3.

Question

Mr Shafto wishes to know the effect on the NPV if the following applied:

(a) Sales are considered sensitive to competition and the selling price may have to fall by 10 per cent.

	£
Sales: 40,000 units at 90p	36,000
Variable costs	30,000
Revised net cash flow	6,000
Present value of cash flows: £6,000 × 3.352	20,112
Less: initial outlay	25,000
Revised NPV	(4,888)

(b) Five years could be optimistic, and three years may be more realistic for the life of the project.

	£
Present value of cash flows: £10,000 × 2.283 =	22,830
Less: Initial outlay	25,000
Revised NPV	(2,170)

Obviously, it is purely a matter of recalculating the NPV using the revised figures for the sensitive areas.

In case (a) above the revised NPV is negative, and there is obviously a break-even point between no reduction in selling price where NPV = £8,250 and a 10 per cent reduction in selling price where NPV = (£4,888). Similarly for case (b), where there will be a break-even point somewhere between five and three years for the life of the project.

Mr Shafto may therefore wish to know which of the following various sensitive areas is the most sensitive to reducing the NPV of £8,520 to the 'break-even point' where the NPV is nil in each case:

(a) initial outlay;
(b) cost of capital;
(c) sales volume;
(d) selling price;
(e) variable costs.

Solutions

(a) The *initial outlay* can rise by the NPV of £8,520 from £25,000 to £33,520, an increase of 34.1 per cent.

(b) *Cost of capital:* calculate the IRR. Look up Table 2. Look along the cumulative factors for future year 5, until you come to the nearest figure to 2.5. The nearest figure is, by simple interpolation, 29 per cent (the table shows the figures for 28 per cent and 30 per cent).

	£	*Discount factor (29%)*	*NPV (£)*
Initial outlay	(25,000)	1.000	(25,000)
Cash inflows, years 1–5	10,000	2.484	24,840
			160

Alternatively, with more difficult figures, the IRR can be calculated by interpolation (see Chapter 5).

The cost of capital can therefore increase by 14 per cent (29% – 15%), which is an increase of $^{14}/_{15} \times 100 = 93.3\%$.

(c) *Sales volume:* the present values of annual cash flows will have to fall to £25,000 (initial outlay) for the NPV to reach nil. Therefore the cumulative PV of five years of cash flows will be £25,000. The discount factor for 5 years at 15 per cent is 3.352: $^{£25,000}/_{3.352} = £7,458$.

Proof:

	Cash flows (£)	DF (15%)	PV (£)
Initial outlay	(25,000)	1.000	(25,000)
Cash inflows, years 1–5	7,458	3.352	25,000
Net present value			–

Annual net cash flows can therefore decrease by (£10,000 – £7,458) = £2,542 before NPV = nil.

Sales: cash-flow ratio is £40,000:£10,000 or 4:1. Therefore sales revenue can decrease by £2,542 × 4 = £10,168. Selling price per unit is £1, therefore unit sales can decrease by 10,168 units p.a., a decrease of $^{10,168}/_{40,000} \times 100 = 25.42$ per cent.

(d) *Selling price:* in (c) we calculated that annual net cash flows can decrease by £2,542 before NPV = nil. Therefore sales revenue can fall by £2,542, to £40,000 – £2,542 = £37,458. With units sold remaining at 40,000 units this gives a selling price of $^{£37,458}/_{40,000}$ units = 93.645 pence. This is a reduction in selling price of 6.355 pence or 6.355 per cent.

It is important to note that this is different from the change for sales volume, because we assume that variable costs will not be affected by the reduction in selling price, i.e. they will remain at 75p per unit.

(e) *Variable costs:* these can rise by £2,542 p.a. $^{£2,542}/_{40,000}$ units = 6.355 pence, which represents an increase of $^{6.355}/_{75p} \times 100 = 8.47$ per cent.

Summary

The percentage changes which bring the NPV of £8,520 to nil are:

			% change	Ranking
(a)	Initial outlay	(+)	34.1	4
(b)	Cost of capital	(+)	93.3	5
(c)	Sales volume	(–)	25.4	3
(d)	Selling price	(–)	6.4	1
(e)	Variable costs	(+)	8.5	2

Ranking is based on the relative size of the percentage change, with the lowest percentage required to eliminate a positive NPV being regarded as representing the most sensitive variable.

The most sensitive would therefore appear to be a decrease in selling price, and the least sensitive an increase in the cost of capital.

This is a fairly crude method of assessment. Criticisms may be that, for example, sales volume is much more *likely* to drop than selling price, but sales price may well be a dependent variable relative to sales volume so that the latter should be monitored carefully in spite of its third rank in sensitivity. Also the analysis isolates each variable, where the effect of a combination may be required. However, provided these limitations are appreciated, the analysis can give management useful information.

Practice

Using the simplified data at the start of this section, calculate for each of the following sensitive areas the percentage change which would reduce the NPV of £8,520 to nil:

(a) initial outlay;
(b) cost of capital;
(c) sales volume;
(d) selling price;
(e) variable costs.

Compare your answers with those in this section.

12.3 NOBBY – PRACTICAL QUESTION 5

Nobby is also worried about the sensitivity of his project. Calculate the percentage change which would reduce his NPV to zero of:

(a) initial outlay (excluding working capital)
(b) cost of capital
(c) sales volume
(d) sales price
(e) variable costs
(f) life of project

based on the following figures.

Annual budget	£
Sales: 10,000 units at £3	30,000
Variable costs at £1.90 per unit	19,000
Net cash flows	11,000
Initial outlay	40,000
Life of project	10 years
Cost of capital	15%
Present value of net cash flows: £11,000 × 5.019	55,209
Less: initial outlay	40,000
Therefore NPV is	15,209

Chapter 13

Risk and uncertainty

In Chapter 12 we considered sensitivity, where profitability could be affected by changes in the variables of which the estimates are composed.

In this section we consider other aspects of risk and uncertainty. These terms can be distinguished as follows:

- *Risk* — Where data may be available to assess possible outcomes.
- *Uncertainty* — Where no reliable data are available, and estimates are purely subjective.

A comprehensive coverage of these aspects of investment appraisal is not possible in this introductory book, though we shall consider below some ways in which the problem can be tackled.

For the more advanced aspects, students should revise or acquaint themselves with the following quantitative techniques: decision tree analysis; probability distributions and expected value; standard deviations and coefficient of variation; and portfolio analysis.

We shall restrict ourselves in this section to two illustrative examples which introduce probability: standard deviation and the coefficient of variation.

13.1 A BASIC EXAMPLE

A firm is considering three products, A, B and C. In the interests of simplicity, each project is considered to be very short term, i.e. less than one year, and no attempt will be made to discount the cash flows to present values. Five separate net cash flows (cash inflows less initial outlays) have been forecast for each project, and their estimated probabilities of occurrence are given in the following table:

	Initial outlay £000	*Cash inflows £000*	*Net cash flows £000*	*Probability of occurrence £000*
Project A	(12)	4	(8)	0.10
	(12)	10	(2)	0.20
	(12)	20	8	0.40
	(12)	30	18	0.20
	(12)	36	24	0.10
				1.00
Project B	(6)	2	(4)	0.10
	(6)	5	(1)	0.20
	(6)	10	4	0.40
	(6)	15	9	0.20
	(6)	18	12	0.10
				1.00
Project C	(12)	10	(2)	0.05
	(12)	15	3	0.20
	(12)	20	8	0.50
	(12)	25	13	0.20
	(12)	30	18	0.05
				1.00

The risk profiles of these three projects are illustrated by plotting the net cash flows and probabilities of occurrence in Figure 13.1.

Figure 13.1 Comparison of risk profiles of projects A, B and C

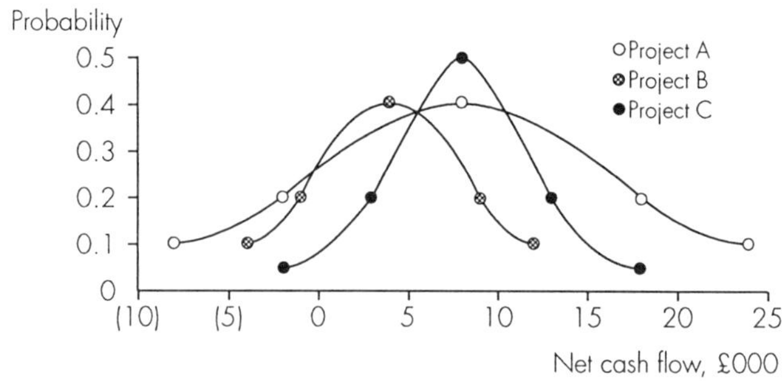

From the figures in the table, we can see that project A has cash flow values which are twice those for project B, and this is reflected in Figure 13.1. From the diagram, we can see that project C is less risky than project A, in the sense that project C has a lower distribution or range of possible cash flows. It is less easy to see how project C compares with project B. Drawing numerous diagrams can be tedious, and the degree of dispersion can be measured by using the techniques of 'standard deviation' (SD) and 'coefficient of variation'. We shall use the data in the above example to illustrate the required calculations for both these techniques, before we consider what the use of each technique indicates.

Project A

(1) Probability	*(2)* Net cash flow £000		*(3)* Weighted value £000	*(4)* Deviation of NCF from EV, £000	*(5)* Square of deviation ($£^2000$)		*(6)* (5) × (1) $(Dev)^2 \times p$ ($£^2000$)
0.10	(8)		(0.8)	(16)	256,000		25,600
0.20	(2)		(0.4)	(10)	100,000		20,000
0.40	8		3.2	–	–		–
0.20	18		3.6	10	100,000		20,000
0.10	24		2.4	16	256,000		25,600
		(EV)	8.0			Variance:	91,200

$$\text{Standard deviation} = \sqrt{91{,}200{,}000} = £9{,}550.$$

$$\text{Coefficient of variation} = \frac{\text{SD}}{\text{EV}} = \frac{9{,}550}{8{,}000} = 1.19 \text{ or } 119\%$$

The procedure for the calculations is:

- Column 3: calculate the weighed value, (1) × (2)
- Column 3: calculate the expected value (EV) by totalling column 3.
- Column 4: calculate the deviation of the net cash flow (2) from the expected value (total of (3)).
- Column 5: square the deviation (4).
- Column 6: multiply the squared deviations by the probabilities, (5) × (1).

- Total column 6.
- Calculate the standard deviation (square root of total of (6)).
- Calculate the coefficient of variation by dividing the standard deviation by the expected value.

Practice

Calculate the standard deviations and coefficients of variation for projects B and C.

Solution

Project B

(1)	*(2)*		*(3)*	*(4)*	*(5)*	*(6)*
Probability	*Net cash flow £000*		*Weighted value £000*	*Deviation of NCF from EV, £000*	*Square of deviation ($£^2000$)*	*(5) × (1) $(Dev)^2 \times p$ ($£^2000$)*
0.10	(4)		(0.4)	(8)	64,000	6,400
0.20	(1)		(0.2)	(5)	25,000	5,000
0.40	4		1.6	–	–	–
0.20	9		1.8	5	25,000	5,000
0.10	12		1.2	8	64,000	6,400
		(EV)	4.0		Variance:	22,800

$$\text{Standard deviation} = \sqrt{22{,}800{,}000} = £4{,}775.$$

$$\text{Coefficient of variation} = \frac{\text{SD}}{\text{EV}} = \frac{4{,}775}{4{,}000} = 1.19 \text{ or } 119\%$$

Project C

(1)	*(2)*		*(3)*	*(4)*	*(5)*	*(6)*
Probability	*Net cash flow £000*		*Weighted value £000*	*Deviation of NCF from EV, £000*	*Square of deviation ($£^2$000)*	*(5) × (1) $(Dev)^2 \times p$ ($£^2$000)*
0.05	(2)		(0.1)	(10)	100,000	5,000
0.20	3		0.6	(5)	25,000	5,000
0.50	8		4.0	–	–	–
0.20	13		2.6	5	25,000	5,000
0.05	18		0.9	10	100,000	5,000
		(EV)	8.0		Variance:	20,000

$$\text{Standard deviation} = \sqrt{20,000,000} = £4,472.$$

$$\text{Coefficient of variation} = \frac{\text{SD}}{\text{EV}} = \frac{4,472}{8,000} = 0.56 \text{ or } 56\%$$

Summary

	Standard deviation £	*Coefficient of variation %*	*Expected value £*
Project A	9,550	119	8,000
Project B	4,775	119	4,000
Project C	4,472	56	8,000

It may help to compare the results with the graph in Figure 13.1.

The standard deviation is an indication of the dispersion of the possible outcomes. Projects B and C are comparable (see graph), but project A's dispersion is double that for project B and more than double that for project C. However, this can be a misleading comparison, because the expected value for project A is twice that for project B, but it is no 'riskier'. The absolute values of the standard variation are not comparable for varying expected values. The coefficient of variation makes the comparisons *relative,* i.e. it takes into account the size of the projects as measured by their expected values. The indication is that projects A and B are both more than twice as 'risky' as product C.

Obviously, the coefficient of variation seems preferable to standard deviation from the point of view of ranking, but even so, it must be kept in mind that its purpose is to measure risk, and therefore it should be regarded as just one useful tool for ranking a project. However, it is not the only one, since, in investment appraisal, decision-makers should look at all the available data before making their judgement.

For example, the chances of project A's cash flows falling below the expected value of £8,000 seem to be 0.30, i.e.:

	Probability	*Cash flow*
	0.10	£(8,000)
	0.20	£(2,000)
Total	0.30	

but there is also a probability of 0.30 (0.20 + 0.10) that the expected value of £8,000 will be exceeded.

On the other hand, project C apparently has a 0.25 chance of falling below its EV of £8,000 but also has only a 0.25 chance of exceeding it, and this may reduce the project's attraction.

These other factors need to be taken into account as well as the substantial reduction in risk shown for project C by the coefficient of variation.

Note

It is possible to set a target rate for the coefficient of variation, If, in the above example, the target rate was set at 0.75 or 75 per cent, then project C would be acceptable, whereas projects A and B would not.

13.2 A MORE ADVANCED EXAMPLE

The basic example in section 13.1 was restricted to a single year and did not involve discounting to present values. Examination questions in this area of risk and uncertainty may involve probability distributions and cash flows differing for each of possibly three years.

In the following example, we shall consider a project X covering two years with three probability factors per year, and we shall calculate:

(a) the expected net present value (ENPV);
(b) the variance net present value (var. NPV);

(c) the standard deviation net present value (s.d. NPV);
(d) the coefficient of variation.

It is suggested that you gain practice by applying these calculations to a project Y, and compare the results with those for project X. Answers and comments will, of course, be given at the end of this section.

Data for project X

Initial outlay £28,000
Discount rate 15%
Project life 2 years

	Probability (p)	Cash flow (CF) £	Weighted value (p × CF) £
Year 1	0.3	8,000	2,400
	0.4	20,000	8,000
	0.3	32,000	9,600
		Expected value (EV)	20,000
Year 2	0.3	11,000	3,300
	0.5	25,000	12,500
	0.2	41,000	8,200
		Expected value (EV)	24,000

(a) Calculation of ENPV

Table of outcomes (£000)

Probability (p) yr 1 × yr 2	Cash flows yr 1/yr2 ×	Disc. fact. 15% =	PV	– Initial outlay	= NPV	p × NPV
0.3 × 0.3 = 0.09	8	0.870	6.960			
	11	0.756	8.316			
			15.276	(28)	(12.724)	(1.145)
0.3 × 0.5 = 0.15	8	0.870	6.960			
	25	0.756	18.900			
			25.860	(28)	(2.140)	(0.321)
0.3 × 0.2 = 0.06	8	0.870	6.960			
	41	0.756	30.996			
			37.956	(28)	9.956	0.597

Continued...

Probability (p) yr 1 × yr 2	*Cash flows yr 1/yr2 ×*	*Disc. fact. 15% =*	*PV*	*– Initial outlay*	*= NPV*	*p × NPV*
0.4 × 0.3 = 0.12	20	0.870	17.400			
	11	0.756	8.316			
			25.716	(28)	(2.284)	(0.274)
0.4 × 0.5 = 0.20	20	0.870	17.400			
	25	0.756	18.900			
			36.300	(28)	8.300	1.660
0.4 × 0.2 = 0.08	20	0.870	17.400			
	41	0.756	30.996			
			48.396	(28)	20.396	1.632
0.3 × 0.3 = 0.09	32	0.870	27.840			
	11	0.756	8.316			
			36.156	(28)	8.156	0.734
0.3 × 0.5 = 0.15	32	0.870	27.840			
	25	0.756	18.900			
			46.740	(28)	18.740	2.811
0.3 × 0.2 = 0.06	32	0.870	27.840			
	41	0.756	30.996			
			58.836	(28)	30.836	1.850
1.00			Expected net present value (ENPV) =			7.544

The above table has been set out in full detail to demonstrate all the calculations. In an examination, the table could be condensed, and some of the calculations accumulated on a calculator. Be sure, however, that your headings are clear.

There is a mathematical short cut to calculating the ENPV.

	EV × DF 15%	*£000*
Year 0 Initial outlay		(28,000)
Year 1 EV discounted:	20 × 0.870	17.400
Year 2 EV discounted:	24 × 0.756	17.144
ENPV		7,544

(b) Calculation of variance NPV (var. NPV)

Probability (p)	*NPV (£000)*	*ENPV (£000)*	*NPV – ENPV (£000)*	*(NPV – ENPV)^2 (£^{2}m)*	*p(NPV – ENPV)^2 (£^{2}m)*
0.09	(12.724)	7.544	(20.268)	410.792	36.971
0.15	(2.140)	7.544	(9.684)	93.780	14.067
0.06	9.956	7.544	2.412	5.818	0.349
0.12	(2.284)	7.544	(9.828)	96.590	11.591
0.20	8.300	7.544	0.756	0.572	0.114
0.08	20.396	7.544	12.852	165.174	13.214
0.09	8.156	7.544	0.612	0.375	0.034
0.15	18.740	7.544	11.196	125.350	18.803
0.06	30.836	7.544	23.292	542.517	32.551
1.00				var. NPV =	127.694

(c) Calculation of standard deviation NPV (s.d. NPV)

This is the square root of the variance NPV.

$$\sqrt{£127{,}694{,}000} = £11{,}300$$

(d) Calculation of the coefficient of variation

$$\frac{\text{s.d. NPV}}{\text{ENPV}} = \frac{£11{,}300}{£7{,}544} = 1.498$$

Alternative method of calculating the variance NPV

	Probability (p)	*CF (£000)*	*EV (£000)*	*CF – EV (£000)*	*(CF – EV)^2 (£^{2}m)*	*p(CF – EV)^2 (£^{2}m)*
Year 1	0.3	8	20	(12)	144	43.2
	0.4	20	20	0	0	0
	0.3	32	20	12	144	43.2
					var. NPV	86.4
Year 2	0.3	11	24	(13)	169	50.7
	0.5	25	24	1	1	0.5
	0.2	41	24	17	289	57.8
					var. NPV	109.0

$$\text{Variance NPV}^* = 0 + \frac{86.4}{(1.15)^2} + \frac{109.0}{(1.15)^4}$$

$$= 0 + \frac{86.4}{1.3225} + \frac{109.0}{1.749}$$

$$= 0 + 65.331 + 62.321 = 127.652\ (£^2\text{m})$$

$$\therefore \text{s.d. NPV} = \sqrt{£127{,}652{,}000} = £11{,}298$$

$$\therefore \text{coefficient of variation} = \frac{£11{,}298}{£7{,}544} = 1.498$$

* As the variance is calculated by squaring the deviations from the mean, the discount factors also need to be squared.

Practice

Calculate, from the following data for project Y, the expected net present value, the standard deviation NPV and the coefficient of variation. Compare the results with those for project X.

Data for project Y

Initial outlay £34,000

Discount rate 15%

Project life 2 years

	Probability (p)	*Cash flow (CF) £000*	*Weighted value (p × CF) £000*
Year 1	0.3	16	4.8
	0.5	30	15.0
	0.2	36	7.2
		Expected value (EV)	27.0
Year 2	0.1	5	0.5
	0.6	20	12.0
	0.3	35	10.5
		Expected value (EV)	23.0

Solution

(a) Calculation of ENPV

Table of outcomes (£000)

p	*CF*	*NPV: CF × DF (15%) – 34*	*p × NPV*
0.03	16, 5	(16.300)	(0.489)
0.18	16, 20	(4.960)	(0.893)
0.09	16, 35	6.380	0.574
0.05	30, 5	(4.120)	(0.206)
0.30	30, 20	7.220	2.166
0.15	30, 35	18.560	2.784
0.02	36, 5	1.100	0.022
0.12	36, 20	12.440	1.493
0.06	36, 35	23.780	1.427
1.00		ENPV	6.878

Using short-cut method (£000):

	EV	*DF*	*NPV*
Year 0 initial outlay			(34.000)
Year 1	27.0	0.870	23.490
Year 2	23.0	0.756	17.388
		ENPV	6.878

(b) Calculation of var. NPV (using alternative method)

	p	*CF – EV* (£000)	$(CF - EV)^2$ (£^{2}m)	$p(CF - EV)^2$ (£^{2}m)
Year 1	0.3	(11)	121	36.3
	0.5	3	9	4.5
	0.2	9	81	16.2
				57.0
Year 2	0.1	(18)	324	32.4
	0.6	(3)	9	5.4
	0.3	12	144	43.2
				81.0

$$\text{Variance NPV} = 0 + \frac{57}{(1.15)^2} + \frac{81}{(1.15)^4}$$

$$= 0 + 43.10 + 46.312 = 89.412\ (\pounds^2\text{m})$$

(c) Calculation of s.d. NPV

$$\sqrt{89{,}412{,}000} = \pounds 9{,}456$$

(d) Calculation of coefficient of variation

$$\frac{\pounds 9{,}456}{\pounds 6{,}878} = 1.375$$

Comparison of projects X and Y

	Project X	*Project Y*
Initial outlay	£28,000	£34,000
Expected net present value (ENPV)	£7,544	£6,878
Standard deviation NPV (s.d. NPV)	£11,298	£9,456
Coefficient of variation	1.498	1.375

Comments

For general comments on interpretation, see section 13.1.

In the case of projects X and Y, it can be observed that project X might be preferred because it has the lower initial outlay and the higher ENPV, but the coefficient of variation shows that it is slightly more 'risky' relative to the ENPV. Which project would be chosen would depend to some extent on management's attitude to risk.

One of the advantages of producing a 'table of outcomes', rather than using the short-cut method for calculating the variance NPV, is that it provides additional information.

For example:

	Project X	*Project Y*
Chance of achieving a 15% return:		
Add the probabilities for positive NPVs		
X: 0.06 + 0.20 + 0.08 + 0.09 + 0.15 + 0.06	64%	
Y: 0.09 + 0.30 +0.15 + 0.02 + 0.12 + 0.06		74%

	Project X	*Project Y*
Probability of exceeding a particular NPV level, e.g. £18,000:		
X: 0.08 + 0.15 + 0.06	29%	
Y: 0.15 + 0.06		21%

Information of this type may be useful, by supplementing the previous information, in he;ping management decide between these two projects.

General comments on the analysis of risk and uncertainty

(a) This type of analysis depends entirely on the assumption that the outcomes for the years are independent, i.e. that year 2 is not at all affected by the outcomes for year 1. In real life, however, this is an unlikely scenario, since a bad (or good) year 1 may presage a bad (or good) year 2. If year 2 is, in fact, influenced in this way by year 1, then straightforward multiplication of the relevant probabilities is no longer valid.

(b) Projects X and Y in this section cover only two years and three probability factors per year. Even so, the calculations required are time-consuming, and suitable computer programs would be desirable for more complicated problems.

Chapter 14

Capital rationing

In section 2.9, we suggested that Bobby Shafto might come up with alternative uses for his £30,000. There may be a number of projects besides belts and braces, each of which may have positive NPVs, using his 'cost of capital' of 15 per cent (see section 4.2).

Let us suppose that there are four other projects, besides belts and braces, which are worth consideration. All six projects are listed below, showing the ranking of the projects by NPV and profitability index (see section 4.3).

Project	*(1) Investment (initial outlay)*	*(2) Present values (£)*	*(3) NPV (2) – (1) (£)*	*(4) Profitability index (PI) (2)/(1)*	*(5) Ranking by NPV (3)*	*(6) Ranking by PI (4)*
A (Belts)	30,000	36,015	6,015	1.20	2	6
B (Braces)	30,000	36,835	6,835	1.23	1	5
C	5,000	6,450	1,450	1.29	6	3
D	10,000	12,600	2,600	1.26	5	4
E	15,000	20,850	5,850	1.39	3	1
F	10,000	13,300	3,300	1.33	4	2
	100,000	126,050	26,050			

Using these figures, we can ask a number of questions.

- *Why does Bobby Shafto not invest in **all** these projects?*

They all have positive NPVs, i.e. they all give returns greater than the weighted average cost of his capital.

There may be two types of explanation.

(a) Internal or 'soft' capital rationing. This may arise for all kinds of reasons. For example, Bobby Shafto's policy may be not to expand his business beyond his ability to control it personally. Expansion can cause problems with administration and control, as well as the difficulties of contraction if the forecasts are over-optimistic, and the dangers of 'over-trading' – a term applied to a business which enters into commitments in excess of its available short-term resources (CIMA *Official Terminology*). Increased sales imply increased working capital, with the associated problems of debtor and stock control. Increased share capital can dilute earnings per share, and external borrowing creates worry and problems, e.g. how could Bobby Shafto increase his existing £30,000 without the problem of finding additional security? The list is almost endless.
(b) External or 'hard' capital rationing. It may be that additional funds are not available. Bobby Shafto may feel quite happy about the forecasts which result in positive NPVs, but his bank manager may not share his enthusiasm.

■ *Assuming that capital rationing exists with a limit of £30,000, which project or projects should be chosen?* Obviously those which maximise the NPV. *How should they be chosen?* If we rank by NPV, we shall choose the following (see column 5 of the table above):

Ranking	*Project*	*Investment*	*NPV*
1	B	£30,000	£6,835

However, we can do better if we use the ranking given by the profitability index (see column 6).

Ranking	*Project*	*Investment*	*NPV*
		£	*£*
1	E	15,000	5,850
2	F	10,000	3,300
3	C	5,000	1,450
		30,000	10,600

This method works provided the chosen investments exactly add up to the amount of capital available. Otherwise, there is a problem.

Suppose the capital available is £60,000, not £30,000. Using the profitability index, the following projects would be chosen:

Ranking	*Project*	*Investment*	*NPV*
		£	£
1	E	15,000	5,850
2	F	10,000	3,300
3	C	5,000	1,450
4	D	10,000	2,600
		40,000	13,200
Not invested:		20,000	–
		60,000	13,200

Project B (ranking 5) cannot be included because the investment of £30,000 is more than the £20,000 left for investment after projects E,F,C and D. The NPV of the £20,000 is Nil because, in theory, it can only be invested at the WACC.

A solution which maximises NPV can be found, but only be inspection:

Ranking	*Project*	*Investment*	*NPV*
		£	£
1	E	15,000	5,850
2	F	10,000	3,300
3	C	5,000	1,450
5	B	30,000	6,835
		60,000	17,435

In the above analysis, we have been considering capital rationing for a 'single period'. However, it is more realistic to assume that Bobby Shafto would have plans to cover his likely capital expenditure over a number of future years. This is called 'multi-period' capital rationing. Cash inflows from one year can be used to finance projects in subsequent years. The selection of those projects which result in a maximisation of net present values requires more advanced mathematical techniques than ranking by profitability index. Linear programming may be suitable for the manual solution of problems with restricted data, but suitable computer programs are more appropriate for more complicated problems. The student should refer to textbooks or study manuals on quantitative analysis or financial management for illustrations of the application of linear programming to problems of multi-period capital rationing.

Chapter 15

Test question and solution

This question is adopted from a Level 3 ACCA Financial Management paper. It is more 'advanced' than the basic question in Chapter 9, but should not be beyond the capabilities of students who have read this book, particularly section 6.3.

15.1 QUESTION

A new polishing machine is required. The polishing machine forms a part of the production process and most products manufactured require polishing at various stages in their production. A polishing facility is expected to be required for as long as the factory remains in operation and no closure can be anticipated. Details of the two machines under consideration are:

	A	*B*
Cost of machine	£50,000	£90,000
Life (years)	4	7
Salvage value at end of:		
year 4 – machine A	£5,000	
year 7 – machine B		£7,000
Annual running costs	£10,000	£8,000

Both machines fulfil the same function and have equal capacities. The appropriate discount rate is 10 per cent. Taxation may be ignored.

You are required to determine which machine should be purchased. Specify any assumptions made.

To what amount would the initial cost of machine B be required to alter in order that the two machines were then of equal financial attractiveness?

15.2 SOLUTION

One of the machines is necessary, and both machines are assumed to be equally effective at polishing. Such a machine will be required for an indefinite period, which we can assume could exceed the useful lives of either machine. Both machines will presumably have to be replaced at the end of their lives. Therefore it can be assumed that an *annual equivalent value* or cost is essential to a choice between the two machines (section 6.3 gives details of the calculations necessary for answering this question).

The calculations of the AEVs are as follows.

Note
Since this example is concerned mainly with costs, outflows are shown as positive, inflows as negative.

Machine A

Year	*Cash flows (£)*	*Disc. factor*	*PV (£)*
0	50,000	1.000	50,000
1–4	10,000	3.170	31,700
4	(5,000)	0.683	(3,415)
		NPV =	78,285

Cumulative discount factor for years 1–4 = 3.170

$$AEV = \frac{£78,285}{3.170} = £24,696$$

Machine B

Year	*Cash flows (£)*	*Disc. factor*	*PV (£)*
0	90,000	1.000	90,000
1–7	8,000	4.868	38,944
7	(7,000)	0.513	(3,591)
		NPV =	125,353

Cumulative discount factor for years 1–7 = 4.868

$$AEV = \frac{£125,353}{4.868} = £25,750$$

Summary

	£
AEV machine A	24,696
AEV machine B	25,750
AEV machine B > machine A:	1,054

Since the AEV of machine A is less than that for machine B by an annual equivalent value of £1,054, machine A should be purchased, if cost is the only factor relevant to the decision.

■ *What should the initial cost of machine B be, to make the two machines of equal financial attractiveness?*

The AEV of machine B would have to decrease (by £1,054) to £24,696.

Multiply this by the cumulative discount factor for years 1–7 (i.e. 4.868), which gives £120,220.

This is £5,133 (£125,353 – £120,220) less than the present NPV. Since the PVs of the running costs and salvage value will not alter, then only the initial cost (discount factor of 1) will alter.

Hence the initial cost of machine B will have to decrease by £5,133 to make both machines of equal financial attractiveness.

This can be proved by recalculation of the figures for machine B:

Year		*Cash flow (£)*	*Disc. factor*	*PV (£)*
0	Revised initial cost	84,867	1.000	84,867
1–7	Annual running costs	8,000	4.868	38,944
4	Salvage value	(7,000)	0.513	(3,591)
			NPV	120,220

Cumulative discount factor for years 1–7 = 4.868

$$\text{AEV} = \frac{£120{,}220}{4.868} = £24{,}696$$

which is the same as for machine A.

Chapter 16

Solutions to practical questions

16.1 NOBBY – SOLUTION 1

1. Payback period (see Chapter 2)

	£	
Total outflow	(44,000)	
Year 1 recovery	11,000	(£7,000 + £4,000 depreciation)
	33,000	
Year 2 recovery	11,000	
	22,000	
Year 3 recovery	11,000	
	11,000	
Year 4 recovery	11,000	
	0	

Therefore payback occurs after four years.

2. Return on capital employed (see Chapter 2)

$$\frac{£7,000}{£44,000} \times 100 = 15.9\%$$

3. Return on average capital employed (see Chapter 2)

Machinery purchase: £40,000/2	£20,000
Plus working capital of	£4,000
	£24,000

$$\frac{£7,000}{£24,000} \times 100 = 29.2\%$$

4. NPV (see Chapters 3 and 4)

Year	Detail	Cash flow £	£	Disc. factor 15%	PV £
0	Machine purchase	(40,000)			
	Working capital	(4,000)			
			(44,000)	1.000	(44,000)
1–9	Net cash inflow		11,000	4.772	52,492
10	Net cash inflow	11,000			
	Working cap. released	4,000			
			15,000	0.247	3,705
				NPV	12,197

16.2 NOBBY – SOLUTION 2

Year	Net cash flow, £	Disc. factor 15%	PV £	Disc factor 20%	PV £	Disc. factor 25%	PV £
0	(44,000)	1.000	(44,000)	1.000	(44,000)	1.000	(44,000)
1-9	11,000	4.772	52,492	4.031	44,341	3.463	38,093
10	15,000	0.247	3,705	0.162	2,430	0.107	1,605
NPVs			12,197		2,771		(4,302)

At a discount rate of 20% we find a positive PV still. However, using a discount rate of 25% the NPV becomes negative. Therefore we can interpolate between 20% and 25% to find a reasonably accurate figure.

$$\text{IRR} = 20 + \left(5 \times \frac{\text{NPV of 20\% rate}}{\text{NPV of 20\% rate + NPV of 25\% rate}}\right)$$

$$= 20 + \left(5 \times \frac{£2{,}771}{£2{,}771 + £4{,}302}\right) = 21.96 \approx 22\%$$

16.3 NOBBY – SOLUTION 3

As Nobby has only £44,000 to invest he needs to choose between the two mutually exclusive projects. In order to make this choice we shall only need to consider the NPVs of both projects.

The NPV of the door knockers at 15 per cent is £12,197 (from solution 1.4. above). The NPV of door knobs is:

	Discount factor	*Cash flow*		*PV*
Year	*15%*	£		£
0	1.000	(44,000)		(44,000)
1	0.870	4,000		3,480
2	0.756	5,000		3,780
3	0.658	6,000		3,948
4	0.572	7,000		4,004
5	0.497	8,000		3,976
6	0.432	10,000		4,320
7	0.376	12,000		4,512
8	0.327	14,000		4,578
9	0.284	16,000		4,544
10	0.247	32,000		7,904
			NPV	1,046

Door knockers are to be preferred with a higher NPV of £12,197 at 15% compared with door knobs with a lower NPV of £1,046 at 15%.

16.4 NOBBY – SOLUTION 4

We need to calculate the lowest annual equivalent value (AEV).

Note: Remember that if the machines produce savings you would choose the machine which had the highest AEV.

	Machine 1			Machine 2		
	Cash flow	*DF*	*PV*	*Cash flow*	*DF*	*PV*
Year	*£*	*15%*	*£*	*£*	*15%*	*£*
0	(8,000)	1.000	(8,000)	(10,000)	1.000	(10,000)
1–4	(2,000)	2.855	(5,710)			
1–6				(1,500)	3.784	(5,676)
		NPV	(13,710)		NPV	(15,676)

To calculate the AEV for machine 1 we divide NPV by the cumulative discount factor (15%) for four years:

$$\text{AEV} = \frac{(13{,}710)}{2.855} = (£4{,}802)$$

To calculate the AEV for machine 2 we divide NPV by the cumulative discount factor (15%) for six years:

$$\text{AEV} = \frac{(15{,}676)}{3.784} = (£4{,}143)$$

Machine 2 has the lower AEV and is therefore preferable.

The AEV of machine 1 would have to drop to £4,143 to make it equally attractive to Nobby, i.e. the total NPV would have to become £4,143 × 2.855 = £11,828. The purchase price would therefore need to fall by £11,828 – £5,710 = £6,118 for Nobby to be indifferent as to which machine to buy.

16.5 NOBBY – SOLUTION 5

(a) The **initial outlay** can rise by the NPV of £15,209 from £40,000 to £55,209, an increase of 38%.

(b) **Cost of capital**

Calculate the IRR

Use $^{£40{,}000}/_{£11{,}000}$ = 3.64 and look along the cumulative discount factors for year 10 in Appendix Table 2. The nearest figure is 24%.

The cost of capital can increase by 9% (24% – 15%) which is an increase of $^{9}/_{15} \times 100 = 60\%$.

(c) **Sales volume**

The present values of annual cash flows will have to fall to £40,000 (initial outlay) for the NPV to become nil. Therefore, the cumulative PV of 10 years' cash flow will be £40,000. The cumulative discount factor for 10 years at 15% is 5.019: $^{£40,000}/_{5.019}$ = £7,970.

You should prove this for yourself now.

Annual net cash flows can therefore decrease by (£11,000 – £7,970) £3,030 before NPV becomes nil. The sales cash-flow ratio is £30,000:£11,000 (2.73:1). Therefore, sales revenue can decrease by £3,030 × 2.73 = £8,272. With a selling price of £3.00 unit sales can fall by £8,272/3 = 2,757 units per annum, a decrease of $^{2,757}/_{10,000} \times 100$ = 27.6%

(d) **Selling price**

If sales revenue can fall by £8,272 before NPV becomes nil, then the revenue required each year becomes £30,000 – £8,272 = £21,728. If the sales volume remains at 10,000 units the selling price can fall to $^{£21,728}/_{10,000}$ = £2.17, a reduction in selling price of 83 pence or $^{£0.83}/_{£3.00} \times 100$ = 27.67%.

(e) **Variable costs**

These can rise by £8,272 before NPV becomes nil, $^{£8,272}/_{10,000}$ = 82.72p, which represents an increase of $^{£0.8272}/_{£1.90} \times 100$ = 43.54%.

(f) **Life of project**

Currently the project will last ten years with cash inflows of £11,000 per year. The cumulative discount factor would have to fall to $^{£40,000}/_{£11,000}$ = 3.64 at a rate of 15% before the project's NPV became nil. This occurs between years 5 and 6. Using interpolation we can approximate this to:

$$5 + \left(1 \times \frac{3.64 - 3.433}{3.889 - 3.433}\right) = 5.45 \text{ years}$$

i.e. a drop of 4.55 years or 45.5%.

Summary

The percentage changes which take the current NPV of £15,209 to nil are:

		% change	*Ranking*
(a)	(+)	38.00	3
(b)	(+)	60.00	6
(c)	(–)	27.60	1
(d)	(–)	27.67	2
(e)	(+)	43.54	4
(f)	(–)	45.50	5

Table 1 Present Value Factors $P = A\,(1 + r)^{-n}$

Future years	Percentage rate of discount																
	1	2	3	4	5	6	7	8	9	10	11	12	13	14	15	16	17
1	0.990	0.980	0.971	0.962	0.952	0.943	0.935	0.926	0.917	0.909	0.901	0.893	0.885	0.877	0.870	0.862	0.855
2	0.980	0.961	0.943	0.925	0.907	0.890	0.873	0.857	0.842	0.826	0.812	0.797	0.783	0.769	0.756	0.743	0.731
3	0.971	0.942	0.915	0.889	0.864	0.840	0.816	0.794	0.772	0.751	0.731	0.712	0.693	0.675	0.658	0.641	0.624
4	0.961	0.924	0.888	0.855	0.823	0.792	0.763	0.735	0.708	0.683	0.659	0.636	0.613	0.592	0.572	0.552	0.534
5	0.951	0.906	0.863	0.822	0.784	0.747	0.713	0.681	0.650	0.621	0.593	0.567	0.543	0.519	0.497	0.476	0.456
6	0.942	0.888	0.837	0.790	0.746	0.705	0.666	0.630	0.596	0.564	0.535	0.507	0.480	0.456	0.432	0.410	0.390
7	0.933	0.871	0.813	0.760	0.711	0.665	0.623	0.583	0.547	0.513	0.482	0.452	0.425	0.400	0.376	0.354	0.333
8	0.923	0.853	0.789	0.731	0.677	0.627	0.582	0.540	0.502	0.467	0.434	0.404	0.376	0.351	0.327	0.305	0.285
9	0.914	0.837	0.766	0.703	0.645	0.592	0.544	0.500	0.460	0.424	0.391	0.361	0.333	0.308	0.284	0.263	0.243
10	0.905	0.820	0.744	0.676	0.614	0.558	0.508	0.463	0.422	0.386	0.352	0.322	0.295	0.270	0.247	0.227	0.208
11	0.896	0.804	0.722	0.650	0.585	0.527	0.475	0.429	0.388	0.350	0.317	0.287	0.261	0.237	0.215	0.195	0.178
12	0.887	0.788	0.701	0.625	0.557	0.497	0.444	0.397	0.356	0.319	0.286	0.257	0.231	0.208	0.187	0.168	0.152
13	0.879	0.773	0.681	0.601	0.530	0.469	0.415	0.368	0.326	0.290	0.258	0.229	0.204	0.182	0.163	0.145	0.130
14	0.870	0.758	0.661	0.577	0.505	0.442	0.388	0.340	0.299	0.263	0.232	0.205	0.181	0.160	0.141	0.125	0.111
15	0.861	0.743	0.642	0.555	0.481	0.417	0.362	0.315	0.275	0.239	0.209	0.183	0.160	0.140	0.123	0.108	0.095
16	0.853	0.728	0.623	0.534	0.458	0.394	0.339	0.292	0.252	0.218	0.188	0.163	0.141	0.123	0.107	0.093	0.081
17	0.844	0.714	0.605	0.513	0.436	0.371	0.317	0.270	0.231	0.198	0.170	0.146	0.125	0.108	0.093	0.080	0.069
18	0.836	0.700	0.587	0.494	0.416	0.350	0.296	0.250	0.212	0.180	0.153	0.130	0.111	0.095	0.081	0.069	0.059
19	0.828	0.686	0.570	0.475	0.396	0.331	0.277	0.232	0.194	0.164	0.138	0.116	0.098	0.083	0.070	0.060	0.051
20	0.820	0.673	0.554	0.456	0.377	0.312	0.258	0.215	0.178	0.149	0.124	0.104	0.087	0.073	0.061	0.051	0.043
21	0.811	0.660	0.538	0.439	0.359	0.294	0.242	0.199	0.164	0.135	0.112	0.093	0.077	0.064	0.053	0.044	0.037
22	0.803	0.647	0.522	0.422	0.342	0.278	0.226	0.184	0.150	0.123	0.101	0.083	0.068	0.056	0.046	0.038	0.032
23	0.795	0.634	0.507	0.406	0.326	0.262	0.211	0.170	0.138	0.112	0.091	0.074	0.060	0.049	0.040	0.033	0.027
24	0.788	0.622	0.492	0.390	0.310	0.247	0.197	0.158	0.126	0.102	0.082	0.066	0.053	0.043	0.035	0.028	0.023
25	0.780	0.610	0.478	0.375	0.295	0.233	0.184	0.146	0.116	0.092	0.074	0.059	0.047	0.038	0.030	0.024	0.020

Future years	Percentage rate of discount																
	18	19	20	21	22	23	24	25	26	28	30	35	40	45	50	55	60
1	0.847	0.840	0.833	0.826	0.820	0.813	0.806	0.800	0.794	0.781	0.769	0.741	0.714	0.690	0.667	0.645	0.625
2	0.718	0.706	0.694	0.683	0.672	0.661	0.650	0.640	0.630	0.610	0.592	0.549	0.510	0.476	0.444	0.416	0.391
3	0.609	0.593	0.579	0.564	0.551	0.537	0.524	0.512	0.500	0.477	0.455	0.406	0.364	0.328	0.296	0.269	0.244
4	0.516	0.499	0.482	0.467	0.451	0.437	0.423	0.410	0.397	0.373	0.350	0.301	0.260	0.226	0.198	0.173	0.153
5	0.437	0.419	0.402	0.386	0.370	0.355	0.341	0.328	0.315	0.291	0.269	0.223	0.186	0.156	0.132	0.112	0.095
6	0.370	0.352	0.335	0.319	0.303	0.289	0.275	0.262	0.250	0.227	0.207	0.165	0.133	0.108	0.088	0.072	0.060
7	0.314	0.296	0.279	0.263	0.249	0.235	0.222	0.210	0.198	0.178	0.159	0.122	0.095	0.074	0.059	0.047	0.037
8	0.266	0.249	0.233	0.218	0.204	0.191	0.179	0.168	0.157	0.139	0.123	0.091	0.068	0.051	0.039	0.030	0.023
9	0.225	0.209	0.194	0.180	0.167	0.155	0.144	0.134	0.125	0.108	0.094	0.067	0.048	0.035	0.026	0.019	0.015
10	0.191	0.176	0.162	0.149	0.137	0.126	0.116	0.107	0.099	0.085	0.073	0.050	0.035	0.024	0.017	0.012	0.009
11	0.162	0.148	0.135	0.123	0.112	0.103	0.094	0.086	0.079	0.066	0.056	0.037	0.025	0.017	0.012	0.008	0.006
12	0.137	0.124	0.112	0.102	0.092	0.083	0.076	0.069	0.062	0.052	0.043	0.027	0.018	0.012	0.008	0.005	0.004
13	0.116	0.104	0.093	0.084	0.075	0.068	0.061	0.055	0.050	0.040	0.033	0.020	0.013	0.008	0.005	0.003	0.002
14	0.099	0.088	0.078	0.069	0.062	0.055	0.049	0.044	0.039	0.032	0.025	0.015	0.009	0.006	0.003	0.002	0.001
15	0.084	0.074	0.065	0.057	0.051	0.045	0.040	0.035	0.031	0.025	0.020	0.011	0.006	0.004	0.002	0.001	0.001
16	0.071	0.062	0.054	0.047	0.042	0.036	0.032	0.028	0.025	0.019	0.015	0.008	0.005	0.003	0.002	0.001	0.001
17	0.060	0.052	0.045	0.039	0.034	0.030	0.026	0.023	0.020	0.015	0.012	0.006	0.003	0.002	0.001	0.001	
18	0.051	0.044	0.038	0.032	0.028	0.024	0.021	0.018	0.016	0.012	0.009	0.005	0.002	0.001	0.001		
19	0.043	0.037	0.031	0.027	0.023	0.020	0.017	0.014	0.012	0.009	0.007	0.003	0.002	0.001			
20	0.037	0.031	0.026	0.022	0.019	0.016	0.014	0.012	0.010	0.007	0.005	0.002	0.001	0.001			
21	0.031	0.026	0.022	0.018	0.015	0.013	0.011	0.009	0.008	0.006	0.004	0.002	0.001				
22	0.026	0.022	0.018	0.015	0.013	0.011	0.009	0.007	0.006	0.004	0.003	0.001	0.001				
23	0.022	0.018	0.015	0.012	0.010	0.009	0.007	0.006	0.005	0.003	0.002	0.001					
24	0.019	0.015	0.013	0.010	0.008	0.007	0.006	0.005	0.004	0.003	0.002	0.001					
25	0.016	0.013	0.010	0.009	0.007	0.006	0.005	0.004	0.003	0.002	0.001	0.001					

Table 2 Present Value Factors — Cumulative $P = A\left(\frac{1-(1+r)^{-n}}{r}\right)$

Future years	Percentage rate of discount																
	1	2	3	4	5	6	7	8	9	10	11	12	13	14	15	16	1
1	0.990	0.980	0.971	0.962	0.952	0.943	0.935	0.926	0.917	0.909	0.901	0.893	0.885	0.877	0.870	0.862	0.8
2	1.970	1.942	1.914	1.886	1.859	1.833	1.808	1.783	1.759	1.736	1.713	1.690	1.669	1.647	1.626	1.605	1.5
3	2.941	2.884	2.829	2.775	2.723	2.673	2.624	2.577	2.531	2.487	2.444	2.402	2.361	2.322	2.283	2.246	2.2
4	3.902	3.808	3.717	3.630	3.546	3.465	3.387	3.312	3.240	3.170	3.102	3.037	2.975	2.914	2.855	2.798	2.7
5	4.853	4.714	4.580	4.452	4.330	4.212	4.100	3.993	3.890	3.791	3.696	3.605	3.517	3.433	3.352	3.274	3.1
6	5.795	5.601	5.417	5.242	5.076	4.917	4.767	4.623	4.486	4.355	4.231	4.111	3.998	3.889	3.784	3.685	3.5
7	6.728	6.472	6.230	6.002	5.786	5.582	5.389	5.206	5.033	4.868	4.712	4.564	4.423	4.288	4.160	4.039	3.9
8	7.652	7.326	7.020	6.733	6.463	6.210	5.971	5.747	5.535	5.335	5.146	4.968	4.799	4.639	4.487	4.344	4.2
9	8.566	8.162	7.786	7.435	7.108	6.802	6.515	6.247	5.995	5.759	5.537	5.328	5.132	4.946	4.772	4.607	4.4
10	9.471	8.983	8.530	8.111	7.722	7.360	7.024	6.710	6.418	6.145	5.889	5.650	5.426	5.216	5.019	4.833	4.6
11	10.368	9.787	9.253	8.761	8.306	7.887	7.499	7.139	6.805	6.495	6.207	5.938	5.687	5.453	5.234	5.029	4.8
12	11.255	10.575	9.954	9.385	8.863	8.384	7.943	7.536	7.161	6.814	6.492	6.194	5.918	5.660	5.421	5.197	4.9
13	12.134	11.348	10.635	9.986	9.394	8.853	8.358	7.904	7.487	7.103	6.750	6.424	6.122	5.842	5.583	5.342	5.1
14	13.004	12.106	11.296	10.563	9.899	9.295	8.746	8.244	7.786	7.367	6.982	6.628	6.303	6.002	5.725	5.468	5.2
15	13.865	12.849	11.938	11.118	10.380	9.712	9.108	8.560	8.061	7.606	7.191	6.811	6.462	6.142	5.847	5.575	5.3
16	14.718	13.578	12.561	11.652	10.838	10.106	9.447	8.851	8.313	7.824	7.379	6.974	6.604	6.265	5.954	5.669	5.4
17	15.562	14.292	13.166	12.166	11.274	10.477	9.763	9.122	8.544	8.022	7.549	7.120	6.729	6.373	6.047	5.749	5.4
18	16.398	14.992	13.754	12.659	11.690	10.828	10.059	9.372	8.756	8.201	7.702	7.250	6.840	6.467	6.128	5.818	5.5
19	17.226	15.679	14.324	13.134	12.085	11.158	10.336	9.604	8.950	8.365	7.839	7.366	6.938	6.550	6.198	5.878	5.5
20	18.046	16.351	14.878	13.590	12.462	11.470	10.594	9.818	9.129	8.514	7.963	7.469	7.025	6.623	6.259	5.929	5.6
21	18.857	17.011	15.415	14.029	12.821	11.764	10.836	10.017	9.292	8.649	8.075	7.562	7.102	6.687	6.313	5.973	5.6
22	19.660	17.658	15.937	14.451	13.163	12.042	11.061	10.201	9.442	8.772	8.176	7.645	7.170	6.743	6.359	6.011	5.6
23	20.456	18.292	16.444	14.857	13.489	12.303	11.272	10.371	9.580	8.883	8.266	7.718	7.230	6.792	6.399	6.044	5.7
24	21.243	18.914	16.936	15.247	13.799	12.550	11.469	10.529	9.707	8.985	8.348	7.784	7.283	6.835	6.434	6.073	5.7
25	22.023	19.523	17.413	15.622	14.094	12.783	11.654	10.675	9.823	9.077	8.422	7.843	7.330	6.873	6.464	6.097	5.7

Future years	Percentage rate of discount																
	18	19	20	21	22	23	24	25	26	28	30	35	40	45	50	55	6(
1	0.847	0.840	0.833	0.826	0.820	0.813	0.806	0.800	0.794	0.781	0.769	0.741	0.714	0.690	0.667	0.645	0.6
2	1.566	1.547	1.528	1.509	1.492	1.474	1.457	1.440	1.424	1.392	1.361	1.289	1.225	1.165	1.111	1.061	1.0
3	2.174	2.140	2.107	2.074	2.042	2.011	1.981	1.952	1.923	1.868	1.816	1.696	1.589	1.493	1.407	1.330	1.2
4	2.690	2.639	2.589	2.540	2.494	2.448	2.404	2.362	2.320	2.241	2.166	1.997	1.849	1.719	1.605	1.503	1.4
5	3.127	3.058	2.991	2.926	2.864	2.804	2.745	2.689	2.635	2.532	2.436	2.220	2.035	1.876	1.737	1.615	1.5
6	3.498	3.410	3.326	3.245	3.167	3.092	3.021	2.951	2.885	2.759	2.643	2.385	2.168	1.983	1.824	1.687	1.5
7	3.812	3.706	3.605	3.508	3.416	3.327	3.242	3.161	3.083	2.937	2.802	2.508	2.263	2.057	1.883	1.734	1.6
8	4.078	3.954	3.837	3.726	3.619	3.518	3.421	3.329	3.241	3.076	2.925	2.598	2.331	2.109	1.922	1.764	1.6
9	4.303	4.163	4.031	3.905	3.786	3.673	3.566	3.463	3.366	3.184	3.019	2.665	2.379	2.144	1.948	1.783	1.6
10	4.494	4.339	4.193	4.054	3.923	3.799	3.682	3.571	3.465	3.269	3.092	2.715	2.414	2.168	1.965	1.795	1.6
11	4.656	4.487	4.327	4.177	4.035	3.902	3.776	3.656	3.544	3.335	3.147	2.752	2.438	2.185	1.977	1.803	1.6
12	4.793	4.611	4.439	4.278	4.127	3.985	3.851	3.725	3.606	3.387	3.190	2.779	2.456	2.197	1.985	1.808	1.6
13	4.909	4.715	4.533	4.362	4.203	4.053	3.912	3.780	3.656	3.427	3.223	2.799	2.469	2.205	1.990	1.811	1.6
14	5.008	4.802	4.611	4.432	4.265	4.108	3.962	3.824	3.695	3.459	3.249	2.814	2.478	2.210	1.993	1.813	1.6
15	5.092	4.876	4.676	4.489	4.315	4.153	4.001	3.859	3.726	3.483	3.268	2.826	2.484	2.214	1.995	1.814	1.6
16	5.162	4.938	4.730	4.536	4.357	4.189	4.033	3.887	3.751	3.503	3.283	2.834	2.489	2.216	1.997	1.815	1.6
17	5.222	4.990	4.775	4.576	4.391	4.219	4.059	3.910	3.771	3.518	3.295	2.840	2.492	2.218	1.998	1.816	1.6
18	5.273	5.033	4.812	4.608	4.419	4.243	4.080	3.928	3.786	3.529	3.304	2.844	2.494	2.220	1.999	1.816	1.6
19	5.316	5.070	4.844	4.635	4.442	4.263	4.097	3.942	3.799	3.539	3.311	2.848	2.496	2.220	1.999	1.816	1.6
20	5.353	5.101	4.870	4.657	4.460	4.279	4.110	3.954	3.808	3.546	3.316	2.850	2.497	2.221	1.999	1.816	1.6
21	5.384	5.127	4.891	4.675	4.476	4.292	4.121	3.963	3.816	3.551	3.320	2.852	2.498	2.221	2.000	1.816	1.6
22	5.410	5.149	4.909	4.690	4.488	4.302	4.130	3.971	3.822	3.556	3.323	2.853	2.499	2.222	2.000	1.816	1.6
23	5.432	5.167	4.925	4.703	4.499	4.311	4.137	3.976	3.827	3.559	3.325	2.854	2.499	2.222	2.000	1.816	1.6
24	5.451	5.182	4.937	4.713	4.507	4.318	4.143	3.981	3.831	3.562	3.327	2.855	2.499	2.222	2.000	1.816	1.6
25	5.467	5.195	4.948	4.721	4.514	4.323	4.147	3.985	3.834	3.564	3.329	2.856	2.499	2.222	2.000	1.816	1.6